"After all the rhetoric and exhortations on the need to teach ethics, morality, and family values, finally someone has taken the time to show parents how—in a practical, time-tested, and thought-provoking way."

Denny Bellesi, senior pastor,
Coast Hills Community Church, California

"I have used several of these stories with my own family and found them to be engaging to children of various ages. It causes them to think outside of themselves and come to a deeper understanding of how God has created us to live together."

David Hadley, administrator, First Christian School

"*Drivetime Stories* teaches me how to help my kids reflect on important moral and ethical issues of everyday life and gain critical thinking skills. It's just the tool I need while taxiing from one place to the next. Why waste those precious fifteen minutes staring at the traffic or listening to the radio when I could have meaningful discussions with my kids?"

Lauralyn L. Bauer, professor, Napa Valley College

"*Drivetime Stories* uses the model of the master teacher, Jesus, and his brilliant use of 'slice of life' stories to shape the character of his listeners. It is a tremendous help for families on the go."

Blake Carter, senior pastor, Hope Evangelical Free Church,
Springfield, Illinois

Drivetime Stories

Making the Most of Moments on the Go

KELLY LINGERFELDT STILLE, PSY.D.
AND PATRICIA WACHTER, ED.D.

Fleming H. Revell
A Division of Baker Book House Co
Grand Rapids, Michigan 49516

© 2003 by Kelly Stille and Patricia Wachter

Published by Fleming H. Revell
a division of Baker Book House Company
P.O. Box 6287, Grand Rapids, MI 49516-6287
www.bakerbooks.com

Printed in the United States of America

Library of Congress Cataloging-in-Publication Data
Stille, Kelly Lingerfeldt.
    Drivetime stories : making the most of moments on the go / Kelly Lingerfeldt Stille and Patricia Wachter.
       p. cm.
    Includes bibliographical references.
    ISBN 0-8007-5840-4 (pbk.)
    1. Children—Conduct of life. 2. Mother and child. 3. Parenting. 4. Child rearing. I. Wachter, Patricia Russell. II. Title.
BJ1631.S82 2003
649'.7—dc21   2002155310

Contents

·····················

Acknowledgments   9

Introduction   12

Part 1 The Keys to Using This Book   21

1. *Blah, Blah, Blah, Blah!*   25
2. *Listening with Your Mouth Closed*   29
3. *Walk the Walk*   33
4. *Got Something in Your Closet?*   37
5. *Creativity and Character Development*   39
6. *Your Child's Temperament*   43
7. *Consistency and Persistence*   47
8. *Developing Learning and Feeling Capabilities*   51
9. *Car Talks with My Grandfather*   61

Part 2 Stories   65

10. *The Truth and Nothing but the Truth*   67
    Brandon and the Scooter • A New Take on the Pied Piper • No More New Dolls • Who's to Blame? • Trouble with Math • Chasing the Truth • Faking Illness

11. *Sharing and Caring*   75

   Friends of the Heart • "Sorry, Can't Make It" • The New Baby • Losing a Pet • Play Date Problems • Kyle, the Boy Who Wouldn't Share

12. *Kind Words and Actions*   83

   Stop Fighting! • Brent and the Naughty Behaviors • Susie and Diane • Sharing a Bedroom • Bill and Roger • Alice and the Bully

13. *Cleanup Time*   89

   Tyler and His Treasures • The Cleanup Mom

14. *School Challenges*   95

   Listen to the Teacher • Sticks and Stones • The Good Student • Christina and Concentration • When Good Kids Go Bad

15. *Responsibility*   101

   Linda Goes Flying • Grandma Smith • The Case of the Broken Fire Truck

16. *Differences*   105

   The Woman in a Wheelchair • The Homeless • The Coat of Different Colors

17. *Children with Disabilities*   109

   Living with a Handicapped Sister • Problems with the New Baby • Amy's New Friend

18. *Doing and Saying the Right Thing*   113

   The "Yes" Girl • The Showoff • The Giver • When Adults Ignore the Rules • The Birthday Party • The Television Show

19. *Beat the Clock*   121

   Sally's Schedule • Derek the Dynamo

CONTENTS

20. *Faith and Spirituality*   125

    An Example for Jesus • The Children Who Lived in the Dump • The Good Friday Question

21. *Standing Up for Yourself and Others*   129

    The Guilt Giver • Dealing with the Mean Kid • The Teaser • Gary and the Girl

22. *Helping Others*   135

    The Stepmother • Helping the Homeless • Monsters in the Night

23. *Happy to Be Me*   139

    The Adopted Boy • Feeling Blue • The Tiniest Girl • The Princess Girl • Luke, the Lanky Boy • Lonely in the First Grade • The Child of Divorce

24. *Too Much Can Be Way Too Much*   147

    I Scream for Ice Cream! • The New Stuff • Meltdown in the Market

25. *Do Your Best*   151

    Play Fair • Tracey Blows Her Own Horn • The Best Reader • Deborah versus the Piano • Race Car Mania • Melissa and the Writing Contest

26. *Safety*   159

    A Day at the Beach • Remembering the Rules • Morning at the Mall

27. *Holidays*   165

    New Year's Day • Valentine's Day • Presidents' Day • Saint Patrick's Day • Mother's Day • Memorial Day • Father's Day • Fourth of July • Labor Day • Columbus Day • Thanksgiving • Christmas

    Appendix: A Special Section about Safety   177

    References   187

Acknowledgments

. . . .

This book wouldn't have been possible without my coauthor—my mother. Mom, you have inspired me, encouraged me, argued with me, cried with me, and believed in me. Through it all we have celebrated our special friendship. Writing this book together has fulfilled a special dream of mine about collaborating with you. Now that it's done, I suppose I'll have to let you retire. Thank you for showing me how to be a strong, beautiful, Christ-loving, intelligent woman. I can never live up to your standard, but I'm certainly going to try.

I thank our precious Lord and Savior, who gave us the gift of this book and of life itself.

I can't do what I do without the daily inspiration of my children: Graysen, Austin, and Ryan. Graysen, your beautiful face is matched only by your compassionate spirit. Austin, you teach me about living each day to the fullest. And Ryan, I love your honest yet tender heart.

Reaching my goals couldn't have been possible without you, Geno. Your support, love, and encouragement have allowed me to achieve things that I never thought were possible. I love you and thank you.

Mike, thanks for being my wonderful dad all these years. Amazing that you never complained about it! Pam, your support and love have pulled me through more times than you know.

I have been incredibly blessed with my friends, and even though I can't name all of you here, each of you adds a special gift to my life. Lauralyn, you live out your faith every day, and in doing so you have given me a wonderful model of Christian womanhood. Thank you for being my friend and for letting Ron be my brother. Sonnet, the songs that you sing can never compare to the song in your heart. Thank you for sharing it with me. Dana, thanks for loving my boys just like they were your own and for being my friend. Sue, your voice of wisdom is always there when I need it. And to all of the other moms at First Christian School—the next one is for you!

Ron and Pam, I know I will never be able to thank you enough for your support and care. I will always be grateful to you and to my entire church family at First Christian Church.

Finally, I want to thank those who have gone before me: Grandpa and Grandma Lingerfeldt and my daddy— thanks for inspiring me. I'll be seeing you one of these days, so save me a place at the table.

Kelly

When Kelly and I were out to lunch and brainstorming as usual, I didn't think too much about her suggestion that we have something special (I already knew that). Since we have always talked and talked and talked, mostly about ideas, I assumed that all mothers talked to their children that way. But I discovered that is not true. It seems that most of the conversations between parents and children center around the necessities of life.

It is with extreme gratitude that I thank God for giving me the gift of knowing, enjoying, and participating with my daughter in writing this book.

I also thank God for my husband, Mike, who will go to the ends of the earth with me because he wants to be with me. Of course, he will go anywhere to be with Kelly and the boys as well.

Thanks to the boys, Graysen, Austin, and Ryan, for inspiring us to write a book that will improve communication between parents and their children—and to tell why that is important.

Thanks go to Geno, Pam, and my support group—they keep encouraging us in our pursuit to make parenting the wonderful time it can be.

Pat

Introduction

....

A Mother-Daughter Adventure

As I (Kelly) was growing up, my mother worked as a school psychologist. Because her work was filled with many different types of human interactions, she often wrestled with a particular ethical, moral, or behavioral question. As many of us do, she primarily struggled with these questions in her commuting time.

During these years I showed horses competitively. Because I rode and trained nearly every day, my mother needed to drive me to my trainer's ranch as well as pick me up. This round-trip took about an hour each day. In addition to these trips, most weekends in the spring, summer, and fall were taken up with horse shows. Often these shows were at least an eight-hour drive from our home. Did we have time to talk in the car? You bet! We talked about regular growing-up stuff as well as issues surrounding competition and showing horses.

Most importantly, we talked about people issues. Although my mother was careful not to betray anonymity, she would present case vignettes and we would discuss them. Since these were ongoing cases, they didn't have neatly wrapped-up endings. They were unfinished, just like our own lives. We found that many of the quandaries had no one correct answer, though that didn't mean the discussions were worthless. Through the discipline of logical analysis, I was encouraged to explore my ideas, increase my ethical development, and learn about the workings of my mind. I was then able to navigate my way through the often troublesome adolescent years using the moral and ethical decision-making skills I had learned.

Today my mother and I are still very close, as is evident by the fact that we are cowriting this book. Although much of this closeness has to do with our genuinely liking each other, I am sure that much of it is due to spending so much time together talking about life.

The Guiding Principles

I still remember a story my mother told me in the car one day about her relationship with one of her friends. I should preface this by saying that my mother is awesome at cultivating and maintaining her friendships; she has many close friends that she has had for several decades. Anyway, she had recently discovered that one of her friends had made an ethically unsound decision many years ago. My mother was dismayed for two reasons: First, she had heard this story from another person instead of her friend, and second, the outcome of the decision had been hurtful to another person. My mom was questioning whether she should confront her friend or let the past stay in the past. As was appropriate due to my age, I was not made aware of the specifics. But even without this knowledge, we were able to struggle together with this ethical dilemma. In doing so, I was able to advance my own ethical decision-making skills as well as feel closer to my mom.

Achieving these goals is what this book is all about, so we will begin by providing you with a framework by which to best use this book. Research shows us that children who are most advanced in moral reasoning tend to have parents who communicate with them in specific ways. The stories in *Drivetime Stories: Making the Most of Moments on the Go* use the following four principles to generate moral and ethical development.

1. Support Children Emotionally in Discussions

When we are warm and responsive to our children during discussions, we communicate the idea that they are valuable and worthy of such treatment. The expression of support during interactions around moral issues may be especially important.

For example, parents trying to challenge a child to think through the moral consequences of some behavior will be more effective if they show support for the child's point of view and exhibit empathy for the child's feelings. In addition to providing a supportive platform for children to confront the moral implications of their (or others') behavior, parents who take this approach also model concern for others.

The larger message we are demonstrating is that people in general deserve respectful treatment. Thus we also provide a basis for moral reasoning: If people are worthy of compassionate treatment, what course of action is best in a given situation?

2. Ask Challenging Questions to Draw Out Children's Reasoning

Parents can enhance their children's moral development by effectively using a series of questions. For example, parents can ask children how their behavior (say, refusing to share a toy) led to another child crying, thus helping children come to the answer themselves. This can and should be done in an age-appropriate manner so that the child can understand and absorb the message. For example, telling a toddler not to hit another child because it hurts the other child may be sufficient for communicating the message that one's behavior affects others. This is an improvement over simply telling toddlers that such behavior is wrong.

Preschoolers with more advanced perspective skills can make the connection between not liking to get hurt themselves and their behavior toward other people. As children get older, parents can engage them in more advanced discussions about how some behaviors are better than others.

3. Reframe and Reinforce Children's Reasoning

When parents take the time to explain their own behavior to children and show awareness of how that behavior affects the children, the parents implicitly acknowledge that children's feelings and viewpoints are worthy of attention. This principle of respectful engagement can be an overarching theme for moral parenting.

In other words, we can respond to our children's experience while at the same time presenting consistent expectations, guidelines, and mature insights. This respect is at the core of morality. Parents will find that nurturing mutual respect in their relationships with their children will pay off in the future. One of the most basic ways to develop children's respect for themselves and others is to respect them and require respect in return. The discussion of behaviors that parents consider acceptable and unacceptable helps children understand and internalize particular standards for behavior.

4. Encourage Further Moral Growth

The goal of moral education is to encourage children to develop or mature into the next stage of moral reasoning. Moral development is not the result of gaining more knowledge; rather, it consists of a series of changes in the way a child thinks. Within any stage of maturity, thinking is tied to that stage. A child then reacts to the events happening around him or her according to the beliefs of that stage.

However, children will at some point encounter information that does not fit into their worldview. This forces them to readjust their thinking to deal with the new information. Our job then is to encourage our children to begin to think about issues that are a bit higher than their present level of moral reasoning.

A highly effective tool for supporting this growth is to present a moral dilemma and encourage your child to determine and justify what course of action the person in the dilemma should take. Through discussion, children are forced to face the contradictions present in any course of action not based on principles of justice or fairness. Even something as simple as discussing the day's events also can involve a focus on the "whys" of behavior and their consequences for other people.

How to Use the Stories

Drivetime Stories is a book you can quickly flip through to find appropriate stories to tell your children. The discussion questions that accompany each story are designed to provoke ongoing dialogue and develop moral reasoning.

Stories do what didactic lecturing and scolding can never do: They make us want to be good. They don't just give us ideas to believe, they show us characters to emulate. They reach into our imagination so that we also experience the shame of wrongdoing—and then the thrill of picking ourselves up and setting things right.

Stories can be the best way to teach character because they impart a sense that life has meaning. Through the power of imagination, we become vicarious participants in the story. We identify with our favorite characters. Their actions then become our actions. In this way the stories can become a dress rehearsal for our own life choices. Stories also provide a wealth of good examples—the kind often missing from our environment. They show children the rules of conduct they need to know, and they demonstrate how this behavior looks in real-life situations.

Jesus the storyteller demonstrates the usefulness of storytelling. Instead of raising a sword to conquer a nation, he sat down in the grass and told a good story. In fact, he told a lot of good stories. There's a reason Jesus delivered his most profound teachings in the form of stories—parables about farmers planting seeds, women finding coins, sons who go bad and then repent. These were characters his listeners could identify with. Jesus used things commonly seen and known by people and cast them in easy-to-imagine stories that took unexpected turns.

Even adults respond better to stories than to preachy moralizing. Think about the most memorable sermons you've ever heard. Were they abstract moral discourses or were they fascinating stories about characters in which you could see yourself? As parents, we can compose simple stories, hopefully inspired by the Holy Spirit, to bring our message home to kids. After all, we are encouraged to read to our children from the time they are babies, and we are all familiar with children's stories that end with: "And the moral of this story is . . ." So, although we use books to teach moral development to our children, we don't want to stop there. The stages of moral development continue throughout a lifetime. It is up to parents to initiate and facilitate this ongoing growth.

As parents, we want to raise children who will be empathetic, moral, and ethical. One way we can help them get there is by modeling those qualities in the safety of our home or car. We have provided you with a starting point. For many situations that your child might encounter, we have given you a few stories to talk about. They are simple enough that you can talk about them anywhere with your child. We encourage you to take advantage of so-called downtime to talk about these stories. Time in the car provides a special opportunity because the driver has to pay attention to the road, and whoever is riding in the

INTRODUCTION

car can talk openly without being intimidated by having someone looking directly at them.

Use this book as a starting point but build on it with stories of your own. Each family has its own concerns and issues. Use the things around you to develop stories that will affect your family in a more personal way. Since we cannot know all of you or the moral challenges you face, we can't gear our stories to your issues. However, you can use our stories as a template for forming your own.

Before you are going to be in the car with any or all of your children for a while, thumb through this book and find a story that reflects an area you would like to address. It isn't crucial that you memorize every single word in the story. It is only important to convey the essential nature. Then as you are riding along, tell the story as simply and naturally as possible.

As you use the suggested questions, the conversation may take an unexpected turn. If the turn is beneficial, go with it. If not, go to different questions. This reminds me of a conversation I had with my sons one night after our devotions. The reading was about remaining true to what you know is right rather than just going along with your friends. After I was done reading, I asked the three boys, "Why is it important to do what is right in the eyes of Jesus?" Graysen had been struggling with this issue, so he pitched right in by providing an example of his own life; it was clear that he understood this concept. One of the twins, Austin, had no such incident in his life at that time, but he loves to be included in any conversation, so he launched into a made-up story to demonstrate his understanding of the reading. Even though it was off the mark, it showed that he had begun to process this concept and was at least thinking about it in a developmentally appropriate way. The bottom line is, "What would Jesus do?" With that in mind, you can always get back on track.

It is always a good idea to encourage a verbal review the next day: "Do you have anything to add to yesterday's story?" This reinforces the story and allows children an opportunity to share any new thoughts or feelings that they may not have expressed the day before. I know that I often need a little time for ideas to "percolate" before I am ready to talk about them. Your children may also need this time, or they may have started thinking down a path that needs to be redirected.

Part 1

. . . .

The Keys to using This Book

This parenting stuff is tricky business, but we believe we can all make it through with (as the Beatles said) a little help from our friends. This book is our attempt to come alongside you and provide you with effective methods to communicate with your child. In the first nine chapters we will give you some guiding principles to throw into your bag of parenting tricks. These principles should give you some of the "glue" needed to make this process work most effectively.

To show you how this method works, I'll use an example from my own experience. My son Graysen recently started kindergarten. At his school, all the students wear uniforms (gray pants, white shirts, and blue sweaters or vests). Much like his mother, Graysen has always been a jeans and T-shirt kind of guy. Before school began, we had some practice dress-ups. But each time Graysen tried on his uniform he would say, "Everyone is going to laugh at me," and quickly change back into his clothing of choice. Other than that, he didn't want to talk about school at all. We knew he was excited about going to school so we were not sure what was causing his anxiety. We created a story about a little girl who was starting kindergarten and had to wear a uniform but didn't want to talk about it. When I told him the story, he immediately protested by saying, "I don't have any problem." After my gentle probing, he suggested that maybe the girl was anxious about making friends.

This story seemed to help Graysen express his fears about school. While I was driving him to his first day of class, out of nowhere, he said, "I know a little girl who is about to start kindergarten . . ." He continued by talking about how he was going to help by being her friend and showing her where everything was so she wouldn't be afraid. In this way he was able to reassure himself that someone would help him out and kindergarten wouldn't be such a scary place after all.

The above example shows how even though Graysen knew we were telling a story that directly concerned him and his situation, he was still able to use it to work through his fears and concerns. That is because the use of stories provides enough distance from the subject so someone can approach it obliquely rather than face it head-on.

While the stories are simple to use, there are some keys to making them more effective. The next section will give you a few nuggets to think about while you are using the stories in this book. In "Blah, Blah, Blah, Blah" we will talk about how to emotionally and verbally get to your child's level so you will be able to communicate more effectively. Communication is the key here, so in "Listening with Your Mouth Closed" we will explore how to listen well, which will encourage further dialogue. In "Walk the Walk" and "Got Something in Your Closet?" we will look at you and your potential personal struggles with teaching character development to your child. Next, in "Creativity and Character Development" and "Your Child's Temperament," we will look at some ways to look to your child for keys to how they will best obtain and retain information. Finally, we will round out this section with the overarching principle of "Consistency and Persistence."

1

Blah, Blah, Blah, Blah!

....

In *Drivetime Stories* we advocate verbally joining with our children. Joining can occur on many levels, including the verbal, emotional, or physical planes. It is a method commonly used by mental health workers to connect with their clients at client level. To do this, a therapist must try to see how the world looks through the client's eyes. From this vantage point, it is possible to communicate in a way that the other person can hear and understand. This connection allows for the best possible communication to occur between worker and client.

To demonstrate joining with kids, let's use a familiar example. When adults want to hug children, they commonly bend their knees and hold out their arms at the child's level. If an adult were to simply stand straight and

THE KEYS TO USING THIS BOOK

hold out his or her arms, a child could only hug the knees of the grown-up, which ends up to be an unsatisfying exchange for both parties. Either way, it would be unreasonable for the adult to assume that the child could physically be on their "hug level."

Why then are we adults disappointed when a child can't communicate with us on our "talk level"? We can be very frustrated when we try to talk with children, because we often feel as if we are simply entertaining them with a monologue instead of having a conversation. Additionally, children seem to have a propensity to steer any and all conversations into areas where they have a vested interest, such as why they need a new toy, or candy, or a snack right now. We verbally and emotionally join with children when we tell them the stories included in *Drive-time Stories.*

An effective way to join with our children is a technique called reflection; it entails simply using the words that they use and talking about things of interest to them. This desire to have someone reflect ourselves back to us in an accepting way is a universal need. When we are genuinely reflected (whether verbally or physically), we tend to be incredibly drawn to that person. This concept of reflection and its appeal is beautifully illustrated in Mark 1:16–18. "As Jesus walked beside the Sea of Galilee, he saw Simon and his brother Andrew casting a net into the lake, for they were fishermen. 'Come, follow me,' Jesus said, 'and I will make you fishers of men.' At once they left their nets and followed him." Jesus used the words of the fishermen Simon and Andrew to draw them to himself. They connected immediately to Jesus partly because he cared enough about them to use the words of their profession.

All children need their parents to continually provide affirmation for them. Children are constantly growing and learning and need to have their new selves reflected back to them accurately. It is the same kind of affirmation that we are seeking when we ask a trusted friend to proofread a paper for us, or ask our spouse something like, "Do I look fat in this outfit?" We are trying to ascertain who we are through the eyes of those whom we trust the most. Our children are looking to us, the parents, to accurately reflect to them who they are. If we do this well, they will feel more secure, rooted, and be more ready to face the outside world.

The danger of not mirroring for our children is that they will look for mirroring from inappropriate models. The typical example of this is teenage peer groups. Teens try to gain a sense of themselves by discovering who they are in relationship to others. Unfortunately, sometimes they pick the wrong models to pattern themselves after.

As parents, we want our children to look to us for models of behavior. This begins now, by your reflection and imitation of them. Reflection refers to the verbal form of mirroring, and imitation refers to the physical imitation of your child's play.

When you reflect to your child, you simply repeat back to your child whatever he or she said. This will help you avoid controlling the conversation. Reflection also shows the child that you are really listening to him or her, while demonstrating your acceptance and understanding.

In addition, reflection will help to improve your child's verbal communication skills. Parents do this naturally with infants; the first time their child makes a noise that somewhat resembles "Mama," the parents jump on it and say, "You said 'Mama'!" This refrain continues in the days and weeks that follow until the child actually says "Mama." The parents' reflections aid in the development of their child's first words. Speech development continues as a child grows, and with continued reflection, he or she will continue to attain higher levels of speech.

One of our friends has a son who struggled with his speech sounds at around age two. Not only were his words rushed, they tended to be garbled and incomprehensible. Whenever we were with them, we noticed that the mother would patiently wait for her son to say a sentence, which she would then repeat back to him. Although she was not aware she was using reflection, she was in fact using this very powerful tool for improving her son's speech. In addition, she was improving her relationship with her son. Two benefits for the price of one!

Parents use the technique of imitation all the time without even being aware of it. Perhaps you have noted that often in conversation with a friend, you both have the same body posturing. This is a natural way of modeling the other person's behavior. It is a physical, unconscious way of saying you accept and understand that person.

When you use imitation with your children, you use this technique on a conscious level. When they are playing appropriately, imitate their play. It shows the children that you are involved with them and that you approve of their behavior.

2

Listening With Your Mouth Closed

....

The art of listening well is not easy for parents to master. Many parents begin talking to their children when they are babies and just keep right on talking. Books on child development encourage conversing with children to enlarge their vocabulary and stimulate their language development. For parents of toddlers this means saying things such as, "Look at that red truck!"; "There is a green tree!"; and the ever popular "Here we are at the grocery store!" Toddlers don't often answer back with intriguing dialogue, so these tend to be one-way conversations. However, when children get to the age when they want to talk about their world, we need to be ready to hear all about it.

If children feel that you aren't listening to them, they will let you know. For example, when my twins were beginning to put sentences together, they often repeated a word in a stuttering-like way. We wondered about the purpose of the repetition; it finally became evident that they were using this as a way of creating a verbal "place-holder." In our busy household, they had a hard time getting someone to listen to them, so they developed this way of getting and maintaining attention until they could communicate their thoughts. We found that with some additional attention and verbal reflection on our part, they felt heard enough to talk without using the stutter-like pattern.

Indeed, active listening is significant in ensuring that our children hear the message we have to send. As parents, many of us tend to feel that we have the one and only right answer for our children. We probably do, but it is crucial to consider how to give the message so that it is received instead of tuned out. Think about how we get much of the information in our lives: We receive it in a passive way by watching television or listening to the radio. However, the most effective way to retain new knowledge is to actively participate in your own learning. For example, students in my psychology classes become involved in group tasks that help them better learn the concepts by using them. When my boys were learning their letters, we would take them to the grocery store where they could find all of the items they could that started with a certain letter of the alphabet. We simply learn better when we process it ourselves.

The image we want you to have is that of gently guiding your child toward the best possible answer. Say, for example, that your five-year-old son begs for a toy he saw advertised on television. You tell him you don't allow toys that encourage aggression and/or violence. A firm no should end this argument and is one way to enforce your viewpoint. Another way to handle the situation is to ask your child why playing with toys like this might be harmful. Helping your child discover the reason why he shouldn't play with these toys will be more meaningful and longer lasting than a simple no on your part.

Not using the second method can bring about disastrous results. We know one particularly passionate father who was eager throughout the years to impart information to his passive son. The lack of response or action on the part of the son provoked the father to redouble his efforts to motivate his son. In turn, this led to greater and greater inertia on the part of the son. Sadly, over the years, the two have polarized to such an extent that the son is partially paralyzed with passivity and the relationship is severely damaged.

Unfortunately, this type of dynamic happens all too often. We know that retaining the parent-child bond is crucial to helping children find their way in the world in a healthy manner. Developmentally all children are going to need to pull away at different ages. But if they know that they can return to their parents and openly discuss their struggles without provoking an hour-long lecture, they will weather the storms of childhood and adolescence much more easily.

I remember well an incident from my teen years that reflects this theory. I had a crush on a boy who was a little older than I was. At one point, he suggested going out on a date, and I was thrilled. Sadly, he never pursued the matter and instead went on to date other girls. This was especially painful because he spent time with friends of mine, and he and I were often in contact. So not only was I hurt, I had to be mature enough to handle these awkward situations. As a result, I felt isolated and confused. One evening my mother came to my room; after listening to my woes, she summed up the pressing issues in my life and pointed out that I must be feeling overwhelmed with all the changes that were happening to me. Not once did she tell me that I was wrong to be interested in an older boy or that I would find someone else to like. No, she listened to me, gave me time to talk, and reflected my thoughts back to me in a way that made everything seem more manageable. Because she approached most of the issues that I brought to her in this way, I was able to connect with her through the rocky years of adolescence and beyond.

If you listen to what your child has to say, he or she will be much more open to listening to what *you* have to say. In this way you can more effectively guide him or her to make better choices and decisions.

3

Walk the Walk

· · · · · · · · · · · · · · · · · · · ·

After all is said and done, your child will look to you as a model for how to live. Even if you are living a life that is dangerous or morally bereft, your child will probably end up following your lead. Ask yourself if your behavior is such that you want your child to emulate it. If the answer is no, you should reconsider the wisdom of continuing that behavior.

The problem with the old saying "Do as I say and not as I do" is that children will often disregard what we say and instead do what we do. This is primarily due to the concept of modeling. Social learning theorists have found that new behaviors are often acquired through observing a model of that behavior. One social learning theorist, Albert Bandura (1986), claims that most learning comes from observational learning and instruction rather than from trial-and-error behavior. An early study by Bandura, Ross, and Ross (1961) examined observational learning. Preschool children saw an aggressive adult model use a hammer to punch and hit a large, inflated Bobo doll while saying "Sock him in the nose" and "Pow." In a comparison group the model played nonaggressively with Tinkertoys, and in a control group there was no model. Later, the children were taken to a room that contained a variety of toys that encourage aggressive play (Bobo doll, dart guns, tetherball with a face painted on it) and toys that do not promote aggressive play (tea set, teddy bears, trucks). The children who had observed the aggressive model were more aggressive than the children who had seen a nonaggressive model or the children who had not seen a model.

Social learning theorist Patricia H. Miller (1989) suggested that although other types of learning are important, modeling is particularly important for explaining how new behaviors are acquired. For example, children can exhibit complex new behaviors after watching friends play a new game or after seeing the antics of superheroes on television.

Our children are always looking for clues as to how to act in the world. We are their models for how to be grown-ups. Research tells us that people who are most likely to be modeled are those who are perceived as having high status, competence, and power. From the viewpoint of children, parents fit all those criteria. As with so many other things, this can be a double-edged sword. We want our children to copy our good behaviors, but they are just as likely to copy our bad behaviors, such as aggression.

Children learn from their relationships with us and develop expectations from those relationships. They learn not just from what we say but also from how we relate to them and how we say it. Therefore, empathy, for example, is taught not by telling children to be nice to others or to try to understand others, but by parents' having the patience to listen to children and children's feeling that they are understood. Once they understand what empathy feels like, they can create it in their own relationships.

4

Got Something in Your Closet?

....

When we started talking about writing this book, we had to face the thorny obstacles of our own lives and the mistakes we had made in the past. In being honest about poor decisions and cranky moods, we came to a place where we felt we could write a book for others who may also have gone down some wrong roads. Frankly, none of us has a perfectly clean record, but we can still talk about moral and ethical behavior and about reaching for a higher level of character.

It may well be trepidation about divulging their own past history that makes character development a taboo subject for parents. When parents get together, they often talk about their children's grades, developmental milestones, or sleep problems. But how often do they discuss moral and ethical development? Many schools stress character development, but what is happening at home? Parents commonly get their parenting information from other parents, so if no one is talking about it, we must not be stressing it.

As you attempt to teach your child character development, accept the fact that you have made mistakes in the past, but be aware that past offenses don't nullify your ability to help your child reach greater ethical understanding. In other words, even though you don't feel as if your life can be showcased on the Biography Channel, you can still do very well at teaching ethics to your child. After all, you will have more influence on your child in this area than any other person in the world!

We don't advocate that you spill all to your child about your past sins. If an issue presents itself you can simply say something like, "This was a problem for me when I was young. I hope it won't be a problem for you."

5

Creativity and Character Development

....

Children have a unique perspective on things. When Kelly was young, we lived where there was a lot of smog. She thought there should be a way to get rid of it. We had several conversations about it, and she came up with the idea of a huge vacuum cleaner that would clean the air. That wasn't a bad conclusion; in fact, I thought it was pretty good for a little kid. I could have told her all the reasons that a vacuum cleaner would not work in this situation; however, I chose to encourage her to think more about the problem to see if she could come up with some more great ideas.

Creativity is a significant factor in the expansion of intelligence. Problem solving is so important in our daily life. It is not possible for us to formulate enough rules to cover every item we must deal with each day; children must learn how to weigh evidence for themselves. We can see this in action when we ask a child to do something he or she does not want to do. We can watch the child mull over the pros and cons of doing what we ask: "What will happen if I don't listen? Is it worth it? Let's see if she really means it." Yes, even misbehavior is part of the creative process!

Our children encounter many situations that challenge their creative growth. For example, activities that encourage young children to color within the lines can be frustrating for those children who are unable to do so or those who think they lack artistic ability.

What do we say about a child's scribbling? The first thing that pops into our head is, "What is that?" However, the responses that will best encourage creativity and dialogue will be along the lines of, "Wow, those are pretty colors you've used. Please tell me about this picture." We need to remember that this is a young child's attempt to foray into the world of art and his artistic ability is really a very tender bud. We can easily nip this bud early and cause the child to believe for now and evermore that he just is not very artistic. Or we can encourage his expression, further strengthening our relationship and the child's belief in himself.

In addition to closing off an important channel of self-expression and creativity, by denying a child's early artistic attempts we may cause a truncation of the child's intelligence. Therefore, it is of vital importance that we encourage every appropriate avenue of self-expression.

We have the difficult task of teaching our children responsible behavior without molding them into "cookie cutters." This dichotomy is ever present in our parenting pursuits as well. There are times when children's creativeness must be blunted because it is dangerous, rude, or destructive. We must then try to redirect our children instead of saying "no" or "don't" constantly. We believe that as children are encouraged to exercise their brains, they will find greater motivation to excel and communicate, hence actually accessing more of their brainpower and enhancing usable intelligence.

Children are creative beings and can often find ingenious ways to work through their emotions, questions, and fears. Graysen is a good example of this, because from the time he could talk, he would playact with his toys. When I (Kelly) was pregnant with my twins, I spent a lot of time resting and was limited in my activities. My husband picked up much of the slack by doing chores such as grocery shopping and getting take-out food for dinner. I remember Graysen working through the changes in our lifestyle with his toys. For example, he would pretend to drive his toy car from the house to the restaurant and back again with "dinner."

You can learn a great deal about your child simply by observing his or her play. Issues that are of concern in a child's life tend to be reflected by a repetition in a theme. Play can be an outlet for minor problems from day to day. As a child organizes feelings into stories, he or she is putting them into perspective and getting ready to move on. Through play, a child can grow, learn, and restore. You can help your child in this process by valuing his or her time at play. For some children this means they want your presence but not your interference, while other children may want you to assume a role in their play.

6

Your Child's Temperament

....

$\int$ ome of the ways children handle things can be due to
their temperament. Think of temperament as the way
children are "hardwired"; it has little to do with parenting skills but a lot with the way a child is from the
beginning of life. For example, children are often char-
acterized as easy or difficult. Temperament describes the
differences in how children take in, evaluate, and communicate their experiences. Clearly these differences have
a powerful impact on the parent-child relationship.

According to a number of research studies, a child's early
temperament is significantly related to his or her later
behavior. For example, toddlers who have trouble adapt-
ing to new situations and who are quick to overreact tend
to have more behavior problems in the school years. Early

temperamental characteristics also appear to be consistent across a lifetime. In fact, temperament factors have been linked to issues related to peer relationships, school adjustment, and even academic achievement.

Although to some degree temperament is fixed and predictive for the future, it doesn't have to mean that a child's future is set in stone. The ways parents understand their child and interact with him or her have significant impacts on later behavior.

Parents can sometimes interpret a child's style of interacting as inherently bad. However, a youngster's temperament is only a problem when it conflicts with the expectations of his or her parents, other family members, friends, or teachers. If parents are intense and ambitious and their youngster is too easygoing, the parents may feel disappointed, frustrated, and angry. The child, pressured to behave in ways foreign to his or her basic inclinations and innate personality, may resist and cause conflict within the family.

Once you realize that your child's behavior is, to some degree, an innate pattern, you can make an effort to become more patient and thus diminish the stress and strain your youngster feels. When you think of your child's temperament in objective terms rather than react to it emotionally, you and your child will get along better. If your child has a difficult temperament as a preschooler, and if you understand and respond appropriately, he or she will probably modify his behavior and may not remain as difficult during his school-age years. Your own attitudes and behaviors can play a major role in how your child adapts and expresses feelings.

Avoid labeling your child as bad or difficult. Labels stick, and not only may family members unfairly prejudge your youngster, she may come to see herself as different, undesirable, or just not fitting in. This negative self-image can further interfere with efforts—both yours and hers—to improve her way of responding to difficult situations and can lead to more serious emotional conflicts.

We bring up the issue of temperament to illustrate that some of your child's traits are innate and have not been caused by you or your parenting. It is useful to consider temperament when thinking about which stories to use with your child. For example, Gary Chapman (1997) has a concept about each person's particular "love language," or the specific senses we use to send and receive messages the best. Graysen's kindergarten teacher knows the love language of each child in her class and uses it to help motivate each one. Graysen's love language is touch, so when his teacher praises him for a particular task, she often rubs his hair. She knows that touch means more to him than verbal praise, candy, or any other reinforcer, and she uses that when she really wants to praise him.

Your children are always observing what you say and do. They are learning how to live by watching how you live. Since their perception is so high, so too must yours be about them. It is especially important to be diligent about children who tend to be quieter with their thoughts. Our twin boys love to talk and interact with nearly everyone. Since they are very verbal, it is easy to know where they are with their concerns, fears, and issues. Kids like this are both easier and more difficult. When parents have had a long day, they prefer coming home to a quiet child who is ready to sit and draw or read.

Another factor when considering your child's temperament is timing. Your child might be more receptive in the morning than in the afternoon. Or he or she may be the most energetic in the evening (luckily I don't have one of those!). Children who are beginning kindergarten or first grade have many things to process in their minds and may need more downtime. I'm not talking about empty time spent in front of the television but time playing quietly or resting on their bed with a book or magazine.

We live in a fast-paced society, but we need to remember that expecting our kids to live up to this pace isn't always the best thing for them. We sometimes think that we are giving our children the gift of filling their hours when we might want to give them the rare gift of giving them time to think. As a wife, mother, and psychologist, I often feel like a shooting target at a carnival. I start running back and forth, scurrying around trying to get dinner finished, homework complete, clothes washed, toys picked up, phone calls returned, appointments scheduled, you name it. However, when I go at that speed, my children become anxious and needy. When I can stop long enough to think about that, I will often just get on the floor and have some play time with the boys. It helps all of us.

7

Consistency and Persistence

....

As parents, we know we should be consistent with our children; in fact, consistency seems to be one of those golden rules of parenting. And in a perfect world we would always be consistent with our children. I picture it something like this:

My precious (read *imperfect*) child goes out of character and does something wrong. I, being an unerringly consistent parent, calmly correct my child and state the consequences of further misbehavior. My child repeats the offense. This time, because I have already stated the consequences, I carry them out. For example, the consequences of my child's dumping out all the blocks after

47

being told not to might be a time-out followed by a cleanup of the blocks. Thus, I wait the prescribed one minute per year of the child's age and then supervise the cleanup. Of course, I do all this without encountering another child's interference, raising my voice, having the phone ring, or any of the other interruptions so common in my household.

In the real world, we do have a lot of interference to our well-intentioned plans of discipline. And indeed, it is good to have a standard plan of discipline that everyone in charge uses. This alleviates much confusion and reaps a bunch of rewards (not to mention a better-behaved child). But much like flossing twice a day, staying consistent is much easier said than done.

The other part of the consistency equation is persistence. Persistence in adults is commendable, but in children it can be a difficult personality characteristic. After all, who wants a child who is persistent in obtaining that candy bar in the grocery store! My children run the gamut of persistence. Graysen is incredibly persistent, Austin and Ryan are middle-level persistent, and my stepson, Kris, is not very persistent at all. Graysen's type of persistence is the wear-you-down type, and indeed he can exasperate me just by persevering with his argument. Anyway, when I am done dealing with Graysen and Austin and Ryan come up with an unfulfillable request, I find that I gear up to deal with ongoing persistence. But more often than not, when I say no to one of them, they say "okay" and go on their merry way.

Parents may value persistence in their children because they believe it will transfer into persistence as an adult. This belief is a common fallacy among parents today and leads to many problems for children. The simple truth is that children are not adults and they need to be treated as having developing minds and hearts. So when children get what they want through persisting, they aren't learning a valuable tool that they will use later on; instead they are learning how to be noncompliant and spoiled.

There is a balance between encouragement of creativity, learning, and discovery and having an oppositional child. We as parents have to figure out where that line is and, like a tightrope walker, walk that line every day. We need to make sure our children know that no means no but also assure them that we will help them in any way we can to foster their growth and maturation.

The important thing is that parents be *willing* to use the same type of consequence every time your child doesn't comply with your instruction or disobeys you. If you are inconsistent, your child will tend to test your limits much more than if you try to follow up each and every time. This is because your child never knows what you are going to do and may test you to see what you will do on any given occasion.

8

Developing Learning and Feeling Capabilities

....

When people start a diet, they step on a scale to see how much they weigh before they begin. Classroom teachers compare a child's reading scores from the beginning of the school year to the end in order to get a good idea of the child's progress. Knowing where they are at the start gives a baseline from which they can determine progress.

The following section should provide you with a way to assess your child's baseline of both learning and feeling capabilities.

Learning Capabilities

In 1956 Benjamin Bloom and other educational psychologists developed a classification system recognizing six levels of cognitive learning: (1) knowledge recall, (2) comprehension, (3) application, (4) analysis, (5) synthesis, and (6) evaluation. Let's look at these.

1. Knowledge recall is the remembering of previously learned information. Your child will show that he or she has learned material by recalling facts, terms, basic concepts, and answers. This recall or recognition of information usually appears in the same form in which it was learned. An example of this is the ABC song. Many adults have a hard time saying the ABCs without singing them because they memorized the alphabet by learning that song.

Knowledge recall is demonstrated in a child's answers to the following types of questions:

What is . . . ?
Where is . . . ?
When did _____ happen?
How did _____ happen?
How would you explain . . . ?

2. Comprehension, or understanding, is demonstrated by organizing, comparing, translating, interpreting, giving descriptions, and stating main ideas. The essence of comprehension is the ability to take previously learned material and grasp the meaning of it. It is the translation or interpretation of knowledge. Comprehension is one step up from memorization and is demonstrated by individuals

being able to do something with bare facts. Consider people who are learning a foreign language; they begin by acquiring basic words and phrases (knowledge) but are gradually able to use the words to convey meanings. If you wanted to determine how much your child comprehended about a given set of facts you would ask questions such as:

How would you classify the type of . . . ?
How would you compare . . . ?
Will you state or interpret in your own words . . . ?
What facts or ideas show . . . ?
What is the main idea of . . . ?
Which statements support . . . ?

3. Application is the use of previously learned information to solve problems in new situations. This is the solving of problems by applying acquired knowledge, facts, techniques, and rules in a different way. Application can be seen in children who are learning to read phonetically. They might learn to read words in a particular reader and, when confronted with unfamiliar words, use the same strategies to sound out the new word. As you can see, this strategy uses a higher level of thinking than memorizing a set of words. For example, children love to hear parents read the same stories again and again while they follow along. They will often memorize the words of the story so that they can "read" the book. However, this sheer memorization cannot translate to an unfamiliar book, so when they are shown a new book, they are unable to read it at all. Approaching

53

an unknown book takes the ability to apply a strategy such as phonetics.

You can see how well your child can apply material they have learned with the following questions:

How would you use . . . ?

What examples can you find to . . . ?

How would you solve _____ using what you have learned?

How would you organize _____ to show . . . ?

How would you show your understanding of . . . ?

What approach would you use to . . . ?

4. Analysis, or taking apart, occurs when a child can distinguish the assumptions or hypotheses of a statement or question. Analysis is being able to see patterns and the organization of parts, as well as the recognition of hidden meanings. The natural curiosity of children propels them to discover how things are put together. For example, our boys love to play with manipulative toys because they can take them apart to see how they were made. Again, this is a simple form of analysis that helps build necessary cognitive skills.

To help your child test the assumptions behind various statements, you can ask the following types of questions:

How is _____ related to . . . ?

Why do you think . . . ?

What is the theme . . . ?

What motive is there . . . ?

Can you list the parts . . . ?

What inference can you make . . . ?

5. Synthesis, or putting together, involves originating and combining ideas into a product, plan, or proposal that is new. This is a creative action in which prior knowledge and skills are used to produce a new or original whole. If analysis involved breaking something apart to see all of the parts, synthesis is the putting together of parts to create something entirely new. Right now, as we write this book, we are using synthesis to form a new creation. Composers, inventors, and cooks also use synthesis.

Some questions that can increase your child's development in this area would include the ones below:

What changes would you make to solve . . . ?

How would you improve . . . ?

What would happen if . . . ?

Can you elaborate on the reason . . . ?

Can you propose an alternative . . . ?

Can you invent . . . ?

6. Evaluation, or judging, is appraising, assessing, or critiquing information, validity of ideas, or quality of work. Teachers use evaluation to determine a grade for students in their class. Psychologists use evaluation to determine the validity of a psychological assessment test. The ability to evaluate depends on making choices based on a reasonable argument; it is an advanced skill that depends on ample intelligence and discipline. Ask yourself if this is a reasonable expectation for your child; even if he or she does not attain this level of cognition at an early age, you can test current ability and use it as a yardstick for future development.

Questions that can be used to develop the level of cognition needed for evaluation include:

Do you agree with the actions . . . ?
How would you prove . . . ?
Can you assess the value or importance of . . . ?
Would it be better if . . . ?
Why did they (the character) choose . . . ?
What would you recommend . . . ?

The drivetime stories in this book are designed to help your child move from level one (knowledge recall) to level six (evaluation).

Feeling Capabilities

A child's feeling capabilities are developed basically by internalization. Internalization is the process of taking information from a general awareness level to a point where it consistently guides or controls behavior.

For example, we taught our children that saying "Oh, my God!" is inappropriate and a disrespectful use of the Lord's name. At this point, when they hear someone say this phrase, they will usually bring to our attention that the person is saying something inappropriate. This simple idea went through a process of internalization to the point where it is now a part of our children's value system.

Essentially, our job as parents is to help our children internalize values and morals so that when they are adults, they will continue to act and respond according to these ideas that have become part of their "operating system."

There are five levels in the development of a child's feeling capabilities:

1. Receiving—being aware of something in the environment. For example, a child might listen to a Bible story being read in a Sunday school class. Receiving refers to the student's willingness to attend to particular phenomena or stimuli (classroom activities, textbook, music, etc.). From a teaching standpoint, it is concerned with getting, holding, and directing the student's attention. Learning outcomes in this area range from the simple awareness that a thing exists to selective attention on the part of the learner.

2. Responding—showing new behavior as a result of experience. After listening to a Bible story, for instance, a child might answer some questions about the story or talk to a parent or teacher about the characters of the story. Responding refers to active rather than passive participation.

3. Valuing—outwardly showing involvement or commitment. Valuing is seen with the worth a student attaches to a particular object, phenomenon, or behavior. This can range in degree from the simpler acceptance of a value to the more complex level of commitment. Valuing is based on the internalization of a set of values, but clues to these values are expressed in the student's overt behavior.

4. Organization—integrating a new value into those values already in place, thus bringing it into an internally consistent philosophy. This is the level at which a person would begin to make long-range commitments. It demonstrates the beginning of building an internally consistent value system.

5. Characterization by value—acting consistently in accordance with the values a person has internal-

ized. At this highest level a person would be firmly committed to this value in his or her everyday life and would become known for that commitment— the value system has developed into a characteristic lifestyle. Thus the behavior is pervasive, consistent, and predictable.

If we combine these two domains (the six levels of learning and the five levels of feeling), we can see how to help our children develop new, more deeply and well-defined ethics, morals, and values into their total personalities.

Knowledge and receiving. This is the basic awareness of read and heard material. You can see this basic awareness in your child by having them recall facts or whole theories. Listening, memorizing, recognizing, labeling, describing, identifying, defining, matching, relating, and duplicating are words that describe this stage. Although this is fairly simple stuff, it is easy to get stuck in this stage. There is enough covered in this one step for children to pass most tests and to act in a fairly responsible fashion.

Comprehension, application, and responding. It is at this level that people grasp the meaning of material. One may discuss, explain, report, review, defend, generalize, rewrite, and translate what is learned. A person in this stage will be able to use learned material in a new situation. He may apply rules, laws, and methods. From this level a person will have the ability to question unclear areas. This assumes independent thinking and is the level at which a child may veer off from the norm in good, or not so good, ways. Because this area is full of potential pitfalls for kids, it is important to keep them moving to the higher levels.

Analysis and valuing. When the activities of analysis are blended with the activities of valuing, we see involvement, commitment, and using concepts to modify thinking. We really need to be active parents in this stage. Here is where our children are taking all we and their teachers have taught them and coming to new conclusions. If we don't take part in this process, someone else (usually a peer) will be there to do it, and our kids can potentially be in moral danger at this point. Here is where we think the value of the stories and parables will provide the bonus of keeping the dialogue active with you and your children.

Synthesis and organization. Synthesis is the act of applying prior knowledge and skills to produce something creative. Uniqueness will be apparent in discussion and writing here. Organization is the act of integrating a new value into one's general set of values. As an example of this stage, consider the act of voluntarily choosing delayed gratification.

Evaluation and characterization by value. Here is where we see the ability to support judgment with reason and consistency in action with the new value. This is the highest level of the affective domain as well as the cognitive domain. At this highest level we find commitment to a model to develop, select, or arrange instruction and become known and committed for that action, i.e., responsible leadership.

9

Car Talks With My Grandfather

·····················

When I (Kelly) was a little girl, I spent several
weeks each summer visiting my grandparents in
North Carolina. They had given their lives to
working with children; for many years my grandmother
was a teacher and my grandfather was the principal at the
same elementary school. He was a beloved man and when
he retired, the school was named after him.

I treasured my grandfather, and the two of us had a special bond. A typical summer day would begin with him
carrying me, still wrapped cozily in a blanket, out to the

family room to his special chair where I could watch cartoons on television. Sometimes he would bring me a bowl of freshly picked strawberries swimming in real cream. After this morning routine, there were always plenty of books to read, a slightly scary attic to explore, and friends to play with just down the street.

By far my favorite times were when Grandfather and I would go out driving in the car. We rarely had a specific destination, but we always had plenty of places to go. It seemed that my grandfather knew almost everyone in town, so we would "go visiting," which has been elevated to an art form in the South. Our car would take us to visit those who were sick and alone and had a real need for visitors. Sometimes we would take Meals on Wheels around town. It was always assumed that our drives in the car would include a trip for ice cream or lemonade. It was also a given that if it ever started raining, we would immediately hurry home because my grandmother was afraid of rainstorms and my grandfather didn't want her to be alone.

I couldn't begin to list all the lessons I learned on those precious days with my grandfather, but here are just a few that are relevant to this book:

- It is our responsibility to have empathy for others by bringing meals, having conversation, or just being there to make life a little better for those who are struggling.
- Love can indeed survive over a lifetime spent together. I learned that object lesson by watching my grandparents hold hands in the car every time they drove anywhere.
- It is good to mix in a little fun and good food with your responsibilities.

I know that while we were driving, my grandfather was teaching me about people and that most of the lessons boiled down to "Love your neighbors as yourself." While I don't remember any of the specific stories he told me, I do remember that our conversations made me feel cherished. I treasure the memories of our time together, and I try hard to pass down my grandfather's lessons about people to my sons. This is our hope for you—that you and your children will treasure your times together in the car and that they will learn something about life in the process.

Part 2

....

Stories

10

The Truth and Nothing but the Truth

....

To the Parents

My husband, Geno, and I had recently married and moved into a new house in a new city. Geno's teenage son, Kris, was living with us, and I was trying like crazy to make a new life, family, and home. We were making a fresh start, and I wanted to immediately begin making wonderful warm, fuzzy memories that we could reminisce about in years to come. Every night I opened my Martha Stewart cookbook and went to work on some intricate dish that took hours to make and mere minutes to devour. Every week I cleaned the house from top to bottom, including every nook and cranny. All clothes were ironed and color-coordinated in the closet, including my husband's T-shirts. Naturally, my compulsion for perfection extended to myself. I exercised every day to stay in shape (and to work off those Martha Stewart meals!) and even redid my makeup every evening before Geno returned from work.

With this need to have everything at a high level of perfection, I was less than prepared for the realities of daily life with a teenager. Over the years we have worked out our relationship, but in those early months my expectations were very high and his response was less than cooperative. In particular, I remember waking up one morning to a crash downstairs. I ran down to see what had happened. There was a calm Kris eating breakfast at the dining room table and a large dent in my hardwood kitchen floor. I put two and two together and asked what he had dropped to make such a dent; he denied any involvement. Pressing the matter, I stated that around 7:20 I had heard a crash in the dining room. He immediately presented his airtight alibi that he hadn't arrived in the kitchen until 7:25 and was therefore free of guilt!

My frustration with anything less than perfection at that time in my life prevented me from effectively handling my stepson's evasions. I console myself by assuming that I would handle things differently today because I am older and wiser (I hope!).

How can we handle the issue of honesty so our words and behaviors encourage our children to tell the truth? This is one of those issues where parents tend to say one thing but respond in a way that almost guarantees that we achieve the opposite behavior. For instance, we tell our children to be honest, but when they are, we either punish them for their misbehavior or we praise their honesty without addressing the wrongdoing itself. Either approach is likely to result in unwanted behavior in the future.

Brandon and the Scooter

Brandon was six years old when his eleven-year-old sister Kim got an electric scooter for her birthday. He was jealous because he had seen the scooters advertised on TV and *just knew* that many of his friends would get them for their birthdays. But whenever he asked to ride the scooter, his parents and Kim told him no.

One day Brandon got his chance. Kim was out with friends and he was in front of his house playing while a new babysitter was watching him. Brandon lied to her and told her that he was allowed to ride the scooter. Not knowing all of the house rules, the babysitter let him ride. At first all went well, but when he tried to stop, he panicked and accidentally accelerated while turning at the same time. Several stitches in his leg later, Brandon promised that he would never, ever ride something he wasn't allowed to again.

1. Why do you think Brandon's parents and sister wouldn't let Brandon ride the scooter?
2. Why do you think Brandon lied to the sitter about being able to ride the scooter?
3. If Brandon hadn't fallen and no one had found out he had ridden the scooter, how do you think he would feel?

. . . .

A New Take on the Pied Piper

The Smith family loved their house in the country, but one summer they kept finding mice. Mice popped out of the trash can and ran across the floor. One was even in the bed when Mrs. Smith pulled down the covers one night. Well, Becky Smith thought that the little mice were cute as could be. She loved Mickey Mouse and figured that the real mice were as friendly and as much fun as Mickey. So when her mother had a man come to the house and get rid of the mice, she hid a couple of them in her room as pets.

Indeed the mice were rather friendly, and pretty soon there were many more mice living in Becky's room. Her mother found out about the multiplying mice and asked Becky if she had purposely hidden the mice in her room. Because Becky was afraid of getting in trouble and losing her mice friends, she lied to her mother.

1. What problems did Becky cause by hiding the mice?
2. What should Becky have said to her mother?
3. What do you think would have happened to Becky if she had admitted what she had done?
4. Do you think that Mrs. Smith might have trouble believing Becky in the future?

. . . .

No More New Dolls

Cayla loved dolls more than any other kind of toy and almost more than anything else in her life. She had a beautiful collection that she kept neatly in her room. Every birthday and every holiday she asked for only one thing—a doll.

Cayla's parents loved to make her happy, but they were concerned that she thought about dolls so much. They wanted her to be a healthy, balanced person, not a spoiled brat, so they decided that Cayla needed a "No More New Dolls" period.

Because Cayla was used to getting new dolls on a regular basis, she struggled with this. She kept asking for dolls, but her parents refused. After a few months of this, Cayla had had enough. While she and her mother were in the store one day, Cayla sneaked a doll from a shelf and slipped it into her pocket. She told herself that it wasn't really stealing; she didn't think this big store would really miss one small doll.

1. What would you do if you really wanted something but your parents wouldn't let you have it?
2. Do you think Cayla could have enjoyed playing with the doll that she took, even if her parents didn't find out about it?
3. Have any of your friends ever stolen something? Did they get caught? Were they sorry for what they had done?
4. What do you think about the "No More New Dolls" time period? Is there some other way Cayla's parents could have kept her from becoming spoiled?

. . . .

Who's to Blame?

Kacie was only six years old, but it seemed she was always getting into trouble—at home, at school, everywhere! She loved to tease her younger brother by slamming the door in his face or hiding his favorite toys. At school, Kacie would trip the other children when they walked past her desk.

Whenever Kacie's parents or teacher asked Kacie why she did these things, she would smile and say, "Oh . . . Satan made me do that." She never ever said she was sorry.

1. Saying "Satan made me do that" would mean that we are controlled by Satan. Are we?
2. Sometimes it feels as if we should be able to blame someone else for our wrongdoing. Do you think that's okay? Why, or why not?
3. What would Jesus say about our blaming others for something we did wrong?

. . . .

Trouble with Math

Second-grader Rudy was having some trouble understanding his math assignment. He finally whispered to Aaron, the boy next to him, to help him. When Rudy did that, the teacher came over and asked him what the problem was. Rudy said he was having trouble with "carrying the ones" in his subtraction. The teacher showed him again how to do it, but it just was not making any sense to Rudy. He was getting frustrated and tired and just copied Aaron's paper so he wouldn't have to struggle with it anymore.

Rudy's teacher knew something was wrong when she saw his paper; he had gotten all the problems right. She asked Rudy to stay in for recess and do some of the problems out loud for her. Poor Rudy! He told the teacher that he had copied the answers and he was sorry. Rudy's teacher told him that she wanted him to learn the math, but she didn't want him to cheat.

1. What would you have done if you were Rudy's teacher?
2. How do you think Rudy felt when he couldn't understand how to do his math problems? How do you feel when you just can't seem to understand something even though someone has explained it several times?
3. What could Rudy have done differently in this situation?

· · · · · · ·

Chasing the Truth

Once upon a time there was a little boy named Chase who didn't have many friends at school. He discovered that if he made up something shocking and said it out loud in class, he would get a lot of attention both from his classmates *and* his teacher. From then on, Chase was off to the races. He started making up bigger and better things and getting even bigger and better reactions.

Chase didn't think he was lying. He told himself that he was making things up so everyone would listen to him. If he said something like, "My mom lets me stay up until midnight every night," his classmates would think he was really cool. He also found out that if he said something like, "My dad let me stay home all by myself last night," his teacher would want to talk to him in a serious way. Chase thought this was a lot of fun, and he couldn't see any reason to stop making things up.

1. Would you like to spend time with Chase? Would you trust him to tell you the truth?
2. What would Jesus say about Chase's making things up?

3. What do you think might happen to cause Chase to start telling only truthful things?

. . . .

Faking Illness

Catherine missed a lot of school days in the second grade because of sore throats, ear infections, and colds. She noticed that whenever she was at home sick, her mother would go to the library to get her some books. Catherine loved to read, and she discovered that she sort of liked staying at home.

However, Catherine also found that it was not much fun to go back to school after several days at home. She noticed that the other kids had done a bunch of fun things that she hadn't been able to do, and it made her feel out of touch and uncomfortable. Also, after several days, her teacher was teaching about something totally different than when Catherine left.

One morning Catherine thought she would play a trick on her mother. She told her mother she had an upset stomach. Her mother told her to stay in bed. Catherine's trick worked! She wasn't really sick, but she got to stay home anyway.

1. How do you suppose Catherine spent the rest of her sick day?
2. How many times could Catherine pull this trick and still make it work?
3. What is wrong with lying to get out of responsibilities such as going to school?

74

11

Sharing and Caring

························

To the Parents

Compassion and empathy seem to be in short supply these days. We have sociopaths who kill others and express no regret for their actions. There are also people who are nearer to our daily experiences:

- Drivers with road rage who demand that other drivers get out of their way
- Competitive parents who spur their children on to dangerous levels in sporting events
- Busy fathers and mothers who push aside the needs of their children
- Insensitive people who perpetuate racial jokes and slurs

The list goes on and on. As parents we have an opportunity to prevent the further spread of insensitivity by encouraging our children to care about others and make a difference in the world.

As I was driving one day with my children, we were talking about what they wanted to do when they grew up. Graysen said he wanted to own a toy store so he would always have new toys to play with. Ryan wanted a truck store so he would always have new trucks to drive. And Austin wanted a car store for the same reason. Finally they asked me what I wanted to do when I grew up. I answered that I was already doing what I wanted to do when I grew up—helping parents to be better parents. As a group, they decided that it would be more fun if I pursued another line of work. Naturally, this little exchange opened up a conversation about doing things just because they help someone else. And this is the purpose of this section—encouraging our children to be more caring.

· · · · · · ·

Friends of the Heart

Carson was a sensitive, caring boy, which meant that he was easily hurt when someone was unkind to him. Connor, one of Carson's friends at school, told Carson that he didn't want to be his friend anymore. Because Carson had always thought that he was Connor's best friend, he was especially hurt by the meanness of the statement.

When Carson was talking with his mom that evening, he told her what had happened at school. Carson's mom felt bad for him but reminded him that he had other friends. She then asked him if he knew of a friend who was always in his heart. Carson answered, "Jesus!" His mom gave him a hug and told him that Jesus understood how he felt when friends said unkind things.

1. Have you ever had hurt feelings because of something someone said to you?
2. Do you think Carson was being too sensitive?
3. Carson knew that Jesus was always in his heart. Is Jesus in your heart? How would you tell other kids about Jesus if they don't have him in their hearts?

. . . .

"Sorry, Can't Make It"

Nicholas had been looking forward to his birthday party for months. He had been planning it and telling his friends about it for so long that they started to wonder if it would ever happen. On the last day of school, Nicholas reminded his friends that his party would be in July and that he would send out invitations.

A week before his birthday, Nicholas helped his mother decorate the house and address invitations. But after Nicholas's mother sent out the invitations, many of his friends called and said they couldn't come to the party.

Nicholas was heartbroken when he found out how few of his friends would be able to attend. He just *knew* it was because his friends didn't really like him. He told himself that he would never go to anyone else's party ever again! One night he was so upset that he cried himself to sleep.

1. Could Nicholas's friends have had good reasons for not being able to come to his party? What might those reasons be?
2. Is there a lesson for Nicholas to learn from all of this?
3. How should Nicholas measure his friendships? Should it be by whether or not his friends attend his party?

. . . .

The New Baby

Amber loved being an only child; she got to go everywhere with her parents, and she never had to share any of her dolls or clothes. But when her mom and dad told her that she was going to have a little brother or sister, she was thrilled. After all, dolls were almost just like babies. They cried until you fed them, and when you laid them in their little cribs, they closed their eyes and went to sleep. She thought a new baby would be much like one of her dolls, except much cuter!

After her baby sister was born, Amber noticed that her mom was tired all the time and the baby cried a lot. It seemed that her mom was always busy with the baby. Amber started to get angry that her mom and dad seemed to have forgotten all about her. Sometimes she wished that the baby didn't even live at their house.

Amber's aunts, uncles, and grandparents talked about how she would have to be more grown up now that she was the big sister. Amber knew she was supposed to be happy about the new baby, but sometimes she didn't feel happy at all!

1. Is it okay for Amber to feel the way she does? Should she tell her parents how she is feeling? What do you think she could say to them?
2. If you were Amber's friend, what could you do or say that would make her feel better?
3. Sometimes it is hard to get used to having someone new live in the house. How could Amber's parents help her get more used to the baby?
4. Do you think that Amber's parents are spending more time with the baby because they don't like Amber as much as they like the baby?

. . . .

Losing a Pet

Patti's dog, Barney, had always been a problem. He ran away every chance he got, so Patti and her parents had to be sure the front door and the gate to the backyard were always closed. Even so, he would sneak around people at the front door or get through the gate when they were outside doing yard work. He also had a bad habit of making a mess on the kitchen floor. Patti's mom and dad would get so exasperated with Barney!

But there was another side to Barney. He would cuddle with Patti, especially when she was feeling sad or mad or tired. He always wagged his tail and barked the cutest little "woof" to tell her if he was hungry or needed to go outside. Patti loved to put him on a leash and take him for a walk.

By the time Patti was nine, Barney began to have health problems. It was hard for Patti to see that Barney was get-

79

ting old, and she started to worry that he might die. "What will I do if Barney dies?" she asked her friends.

1. Have any of your friends had a pet that died? What did you do or say to comfort them? Was it easy?
2. What would you want your friends to do or say if your pet died?

. . . .

Play Date Problems

One day Kendrick went over to his friend Jake's house to play. He had a great time playing with Jake's toys. During the day he kept finding more and more toys in Jake's closet, under his bed, and even in his dresser drawers. But in all of Kendrick's excitement, he forgot that he should be putting things back after he was done playing with them. When Kendrick's mom came to pick him up, she was shocked to find that Jake's room was a complete disaster. She made Kendrick get everything organized, cleaned up, and put back again so that Jake's room looked the same as when Kendrick had arrived that morning.

1. Would you do things at someone else's house that you would not do at home? What kinds of things?
2. Have you ever had a friend come over and leave a mess for you to clean up? How would you like your room to look when you and your friends were done playing?
3. What could you do to make sure you have time to clean up before your play date is over?

Kyle, the Boy Who Wouldn't Share

Kyle was an only child, and his parents made sure he had the newest and best of everything. This included toys, videotapes, games, and even his very own computer. Everything ran smoothly as long as Kyle's mom was available to play with him and he was entertained. However, whenever Kyle had a friend at his house, things got out of hand. The problem was that Kyle had a hard time letting others play with his toys. When a friend would pick up a toy, Kyle would grab the toy out of his hands and yell things like, "Put that back. It's mine. Don't touch it!" Before the visit was over, Kyle would accuse the other child of planning to take his toys home and keep them. Needless to say, Kyle didn't have friends over very often.

1. What would you tell Kyle about playing with friends and sharing his toys?
2. What do you think Kyle's mom and dad could have done differently?
3. What would you think of a boy who had all the toys he wanted but wouldn't share them? Would you want to play with him?

12

Kind Words and Actions

....

To the Parents

The title of this chapter comes from one of the most important house rules in our home. We believe that our home should be an oasis from the rest of the world, a safe place where we can rejuvenate ourselves and be encouraged by the love and support of our family. I know it sounds idealistic and we only get there on occasion, but we are always working toward that goal. Having a rule about kind words and actions helps maintain that purpose and keeps our eyes on the goal.

We had an opportunity to talk about kind words the other day. Someone had made an unkind remark about me, and I was hurt by it. Graysen could see that I was troubled and asked me about it. Without specifying what had been said, I told him the story. He connected with it and talked about how some kids at school would say mean things when other kids didn't finish their work quickly or well. This conversation accomplished two things. One, he understood why I was unhappy and that it wasn't his fault. Two, the principle of using kind words was reinforced for him.

·······

Stop Fighting!

Jessie loved her parents very much and knew that her parents loved her too. Sometimes, though, she wondered whether or not her parents still loved each other. It just seemed like every time they were together, they were either really quiet or they were arguing. She didn't really understand why they were fighting.

Jessie didn't want her friends to be around when her parents were arguing, so she stopped inviting friends over to play at her house. She tried not to be home much herself and went to friends' houses as much as possible. When she was home, she usually went to her room to play quietly or read, because she didn't want to do anything to make her parents angrier.

1. Was there someone Jessie could have talked to about her parents?
2. If you were Jessie's friend, what would you tell her?

3. Do you think that Jessie should have told her parents how frightened she was when they argued?

·······

Brent and the Naughty Behaviors

Brent was learning so much in his first-grade classroom, but some of it wasn't the right kind of stuff to learn. He was learning that some children talk back, cry, and whine when they don't get their way, and refuse to obey adults! Because Brent had always been a well-behaved child, he was surprised to see other children acting in this way. He wondered if he might be missing out on something by always being obedient to his parents. He decided to try out some of these different ways of behaving and see what might happen as a result.

So the next time Brent's mother asked him to put on his shoes because they were going to the grocery store, he yelled "no" at her and stomped into his room. And when his father told him to turn off the television because it was time for dinner, he pretended that he couldn't hear. Brent even extended his experiment to school, and when his teacher wanted him to do a hard problem on the board, he burst into tears.

1. What do you think Brent's parents thought about his behavior?
2. Do you think Brent's parents should punish him?
3. What should Brent's parents do when he disobeys them?
4. What might Jesus think about how Brent is acting?

Susie and Diane

One day when Susie and her new friend, Diane, were walking to school, Diane spotted a small purse on the ground. She bent down and picked it up. "Look what I found! And there's money in it too!" she exclaimed.

"Wait, Diane," Susie said. "That belongs to someone else. We need to return it to the owner! Let's see if anyone from our school lost it."

Diane said, "No way! Finders keepers!"

1. What would you do if you found a purse with money in it?
2. What does *finders keepers* mean?
3. What could Susie do about making sure the purse is returned to whoever lost it?
4. Would you want to have a friend like Diane?

· · · · · · ·

Sharing a Bedroom

Sharon and Katie had to share a bedroom. Their brothers had to share a room as well. Sharon and Katie were loving sisters—most of the time.

When Katie was getting ready for church one Sunday, she saw a hair clip that Sharon had recently received for her birthday. Since Sharon had nursery duty and had already left for church, Katie tried it in her hair. It looked good to Katie, so she left it in and forgot about it.

Later, when Sharon noticed her hair clip on Katie, she was boiling mad! One of the house rules about sharing a room was to not use anything that belonged to the other without permission. Sharon went right to her mother and complained loudly that Katie was always taking her things without permission!

1. Did Katie do something wrong or did she just make a mistake?
2. What do you think the girls' mother should do?
3. What would you do if you were Katie?
4. What are some other problems with sharing a room? What are some good things?

. . . .

Bill and Roger

As a reward for learning his numbers from one to a hundred, Bill's teacher gave him a special colored pencil. Because Roger hadn't earned a special pencil, he was feeling jealous of Bill. So, as their teacher was writing on the board, Roger reached over and took Bill's pencil. Bill saw Roger take it and politely asked him to return the pencil. Roger thought that he might be able to get Bill into trouble, so he just grinned in a mean way and shook his head. Bill was getting frustrated, so he again asked Roger to return the pencil, this time in a much louder voice. The teacher heard him and turned around.

1. Who do you think got into trouble—Bill for speaking out loud in class without raising his hand or Roger for taking Bill's special pencil?
2. How else could Bill have handled this situation?

3. What could Roger have done to get his own special pencil? Why do you think Roger acted the way he did?

. . . .

Alice and the Bully

Alice got along well with her friends at school. However, one day a new boy came up to her and demanded her lunch money. Alice was so startled that she gave it to him. The next day he told her that he wanted her lunch money again. When she told him "No" he said that if she didn't give it to him he would tell everyone she was a mean person. Alice wanted everyone to think that she was nice, so to keep the boy from telling stories about her, she gave him the money. The boy told her that from now on, she would have to give him her lunch money every day or he would tell mean stories about her to all of her friends.

1. What do you think happened then?
2. What are some things Alice could do? How do you think Alice could keep her lunch money?
3. Would Alice's friends believe that she was mean just because the new boy told stories about her?
3. Who could Alice talk to about the bully?

13

Cleanup Time

....

To the Parents

While at the University of California Davis Medical Center Department of Pediatrics, I (Kelly) worked with children and the adults who cared for them. Regardless of who was taking care of the child—parents, foster parent, or relative—I always used a baseline assessment of parenting skills to determine progress during treatment. Part of my initial assessment was asking the caretaker to tell the child to clean up the toys he or she had played with in the room.

Cleanup time was an exercise to determine the relationship between child and caretaker. Some caretakers would put away the toys themselves; in that case, I would ask the caretaker to purposely make a mess for the child to clean up. Other caretakers were unable to persuade their child to clean up the mess. In any case, this five-minute exercise provided me with a good snapshot that I could use for the rest of the therapeutic relationship.

I often need to remind myself to insist that my own children clean up. As a busy parent, I find it easier and faster to do this myself. But doing this only accomplishes a short-term gain, rather than the long-term gain of teaching my child responsibility. For me, it comes down to stopping just long enough to let the boys clear the table, pick up their toys, or do any other developmentally appropriate tasks. Use whatever method works for you to get your child to clean up.

Since children gain much of their self-image from their family, we encourage having regular family team meetings; these provide a structure in which a family can further strengthen and expand its relationship.

Team meetings also enable families to set up a framework in which everyone shares responsibility for running the house. In many homes Mom has ownership of all the chores. However, if all the members take ownership of their responsibilities in the family, they will soon develop pride in being able to manage their own corner of the house. Every member, young or old, should be able to take on something that will enable them to feel like a partner in the family.

Here's how to implement a family team meeting:

Step One—Pick a time when everyone is home: after dinner, Sunday evening, Saturday morning—any time that you can be fairly sure you can manage every week.

Step Two—To introduce the concept, the moderator asks questions such as: "How do we, as a family, want to present ourselves to one another and to the world? Do we want trash to be lying around? Do we want the yard to be messy? Who is to cook? Who is to clean? Who is to provide money for us?" The questions will vary according to the home, but the idea is to realize how much goes into the making of a smoothly running home.

Step Three—Each family member makes two lists. The first will include personal responsibilities such as making one's own bed, cleaning up one's own space, and completing homework. The second list will include a family member's responsibilities to the home, such as feeding the dog, emptying the dishwasher, and putting away folded laundry. Parents may list going to work to bring in money for the home, paying bills, cooking, and carpooling.

Step Four—Each person reads his or her lists. The moderator then makes a list of all the things everyone has agreed are necessary to achieve the desired standard of living.

Even young children can help with such duties as setting and clearing the table at mealtime; washing and drying dishes; weeding flowerbeds; and taking out the trash.

Each family member then makes a third list of whatever jobs he thinks he can manage to do.

Step Five—After each family member has agreed on his or her tasks for the next week, the moderator should post the list for each person to review. Duties should be checked off as they are completed.

. . . .

Tyler and His Treasures

When Tyler was three, he loved fire trucks; when he was four, he loved construction vehicles. When he turned five, dinosaurs were his favorite. He had a huge collection of toys that cluttered up the room he shared with his brothers.

One summer, Tyler's family moved to a larger house. Tyler was excited—he wouldn't have to share a room with his two brothers anymore! Tyler's grandparents invited Tyler and his brothers to stay with them for a few days so their mom and dad could get the new house settled. Tyler's mother planned to organize his room so that when he moved in everything would be in place.

Tyler's grandmother suggested to Tyler that maybe he should organize at least part of the room himself. Tyler's mother agreed, and although she put his bed, dresser, and bookcase where she wanted them, she set aside his special collection of toys for him to put away. The day Tyler came home, he spent the whole afternoon putting his treasures exactly where he wanted them.

1. Would it have been easier for Tyler's mother to just put away his treasures for him? Do you think she should have? Why, or why not?
2. What did Tyler learn from putting away his own toys?
3. Is there another way you would like to organize your room?

....

The Cleanup Mom

Jeff and Katie's mom was a schoolteacher and loved to have everything in order—at school *and* at home. She always packed Jeff and Katie's school lunches the night before, laid out their clothes for the next morning, and set out their breakfast dishes. After school, she did laundry and made dinner, which was always on the table by 5:30 and cleared by 6:00.

This schedule made things very simple for Jeff and Katie, but it seemed to them that their mom didn't have time for them. They hardly dared ask her for help with their homework because every night after dinner she was busy grading her students' papers. Jeff and Katie's dad worked almost every evening, so he didn't spend much time with them either.

1. What do you think is the main problem with Jeff and Katie's family?
2. What responsibilities did Jeff and Katie have at home?
3. Do you think it's more important for parents to do things *for* their children or *with* their children? Why?

14

School Challenges

....

To the Parents

You've probably heard it before: You are your child's first teacher. And not only are you your child's first teacher, you are also his or her most important teacher. Think about how much your child has learned up to now—crawling, sitting up, standing, walking, talking. Take a moment now to congratulate yourself on teaching your child these incredible skills (as parents, we need to take some credit now and again).

Now you have sent your child out into the world to be taught by others. You know that there are bound to be some difficulties and problem areas that will pop up during the school years. How best to handle them? We suggest that you continue to talk with your child about anything and everything that happens to them at school. We also suggest that you try to maintain communication and a spirit of partnership with your child's teacher. This two-pronged approach will be the best way to navigate the sometimes rough waters of elementary school.

· · · · · · ·

Listen to the Teacher

Brian was in the first grade. Even though he liked his teacher, Mrs. Bramwell, he often thought about things other than schoolwork when he was in class. For example, Brian had received a really cool airplane for his birthday.

One afternoon in class he was daydreaming about the plane and about being a pilot when Mrs. Bramwell asked him to answer the question on the board. Brian should have known the answer, but he hadn't been paying attention so he didn't even know the question. Instead of telling Mrs. Bramwell he hadn't been listening he just stared at her.

1. Do you ever daydream in class? What's wrong with daydreaming?
2. What do you think Mrs. Bramwell could do to get Brian to pay attention a little better?

· · · · · · ·

Sticks and Stones

One morning, the kindergarteners and first- and second-graders were playing outside during recess. Iris, one of the kindergarteners, was playing with some of the second-grade girls.

The older girls dared Iris to call Cassie, another girl in kindergarten, ugly and stupid. Wanting to fit in with the older crowd, Iris did what they said. Cassie burst into tears and ran to tell the teacher.

1. Has anyone ever called you a name? How did you feel?
2. What would make Iris be cruel to one of her classmates?
3. What should Iris's teacher do?

. . . .

The Good Student

Sammy was a good student in the second grade. He had always taken his schoolwork seriously and done a good job. However, because he got good grades, people expected a lot of him. Even Sammy's teacher expected him to do advanced work.

Sammy did as well as he could, but he was puzzled by these high expectations of him. Sometimes he thought he couldn't be good enough to please everyone. He also wondered if his teachers and parents would still like him if he just did an okay job instead of an outstanding one.

1. What do you think Sammy's parents are saying to him about meeting other people's expectations?
2. Do you ever feel that people are expecting too much of you? What can you do about that?
3. Do you think that Sammy would feel better if he remembers that Jesus loves him just as he is, no matter what kind of grades he gets?

Christina and Concentration

Christina got along well with almost all the kids in her fourth-grade class. Recess and lunch time were her favorite times of the day because she could sit and talk with her friends. Christina knew she wasn't supposed to talk with them during class, but she couldn't help it; it was hard to concentrate when her friends were all around her. She kept thinking of things she had to tell them. Several times throughout the day, her teacher had to ask her to "stay on task."

Christina's teacher called a meeting with her parents, and the three of them sat down with Christina and talked about possible solutions to the problem. The teacher suggested moving Christina to the other fourth-grade class. This upset Christina; she promised she'd try really hard to concentrate in class.

1. What do you think of the teacher's suggestion?
2. What might be some other solutions to the problem?
3. What do you think Christina's parents could do that would help her to concentrate better? What could Christina do?

. . . .

When Good Kids Go Bad

Maria was in the fourth grade and always got along well with the other kids, but lately she had become disruptive. She bothered the other kids during work time, talked out of turn, and even fell off her chair on purpose sometimes.

Maria also caused trouble on the playground at recess time; she called her classmates names and pestered the younger kids. No one liked the "new" Maria very much. They wanted the "old" Maria back.

1. If you were in Maria's class, what would you say to her?
2. What could be the cause of Maria's change in behavior?
3. What could Maria do to win her friends back?

15

Responsibility

....

To the Parents

When I became a parent, I was awestruck by the immense responsibility in being a mother. Overnight I was responsible for meeting every need of this tiny baby. Each decision I made was weighed by how it would affect my precious angel. I was now on call twenty-four hours every day, and there was no time off for good behavior. Frankly, the demands of every job I had ever held paled in comparison to this one.

This overwhelming responsibility was emphasized for me one day when my child was only a few weeks old. He was taking a nap and I was thinking about starting dinner. I needed a few items for a recipe and began to put on my shoes to go to the store. It came as a shock to me when

I suddenly realized that because there was a baby in the other room, I couldn't just scamper down to the store anymore!

Parents must teach their children about responsibility. Hopefully, as they mature, our children will become more and more responsible for themselves. This is a long process, and sometimes we may think we are taking steps backward instead of forward. Whenever we feel discouraged about this task, remember our long-term goal—raising children who will become responsible members of society. We hope the following stories will help you in this quest.

· · · · · · ·

Linda Goes Flying

Linda's family decided to go to Florida for spring vacation. Linda had an older sister and a younger brother, so with the five of them going, a lot needed to be done ahead of time.

At their family meeting, Linda's parents decided each child could bring one suitcase and one backpack for the trip. All three children had to pack their own luggage and attach their own luggage tags. One week before the trip, Linda's brother and sister had their bags packed and ready to go. Linda thought it was silly to pack that early, so she waited until the night before they were to leave on their vacation. She threw her favorite clothes into the suitcase and put some toys and books into her backpack. She was ready.

On the morning of the trip, Linda's family arrived at the airport, checked their luggage, and boarded the plane.

Upon landing in Orlando, they went to claim their luggage; all their suitcases came around on the carousel. All of them except Linda's.

1. What do you think might have happened to Linda's suitcase?
2. What does the word *procrastination* mean? Do you think Linda might have procrastinated in getting ready for the trip?
3. What could Linda have done differently to make the trip go more smoothly?

. . . .

Grandma Smith

Dana loved living near her Grandma Smith. The two of them spent a lot of time together baking cookies and playing board games. Everything changed when Dana's grandma became ill.

Because Dana's mother had to take care of Grandma Smith most of the time, she couldn't help in the classroom at Dana's school like some of the other mothers. It also meant that emergency calls late at night or early in the morning resulted in Dana's mother having to rush out to take care of Grandma Smith.

Dana loved her mother and grandmother very much, but sometimes she was frustrated when her plans had to be canceled because of Grandma Smith's illness. And sometimes, when her mom was gone, Dana had to help her dad with chores.

1. How could Dana help her mother?

2. What could Dana do for her grandmother?

3. What can you do to help people who are sick?

· · · · · · ·

The Case of the Broken Fire Truck

Max and Kevin were brothers and liked the same kind of toys, mostly trucks, cars, and airplanes. One day Max accidentally broke one of Kevin's favorite fire trucks. He knew that Kevin would find out, and he was really worried that Kevin would be angry. Max wondered if he should hide the broken truck somewhere so Kevin would just think he had lost it. He also thought about blaming someone else for breaking the truck. Then he considered simply denying that he had any knowledge whatsoever about the damaged truck.

On the other hand, Max knew that he should be honest about breaking the fire truck. But Kevin would still get mad and his parents would probably punish him. He didn't know what to do.

1. What do you think Max should do about the broken fire truck?

2. Do you think Max should tell his parents about the broken toy or should he just keep it between himself and Kevin?

3. What do you think Jesus would want Max to do in this case?

16

Differences

······················

To the Parents

Some differences among people are readily apparent, such as hair, eye, and skin color. Other differences are less easy to detect; people have varying family of origin experiences, religious beliefs, and social status. The vast array of differences among people can provide wonderful opportunities for learning about each other. For parents, the challenge is to raise children who are open to others without prejudice or pre-judgment.

By about four years of age, children are aware of differences among people, primarily in characteristics like appearance, language, and names. Later they are aware of religious and cultural distinctions as well. To some extent, children begin to define themselves through their understanding of these personal differences. This can turn into an appreciation for others or, unfortunately, pre-prejudice: misconceptions, discomfort, fear, and rejection of differences that can easily blossom into full-fledged prejudice.

We cannot ignore the prejudice to which our children may be exposed in the media or in their own experience. We serve as the most powerful influence and role models for our youngsters. More than anyone else, parents can mold children's attitudes and behaviors toward others.

Our actions toward the people in our lives will lay the foundation for how our children relate to their peers and others. In doing this it is important for us to examine our attitudes and the way we feel about people with traits and characteristics different from our own. If we want our children to be free of prejudice, we must demonstrate that attitude in our words and deeds.

When you sense that your youngster has negative attitudes toward others, or witness or hear about any intolerant or discriminatory behavior on his or her part, do not ignore it; discuss it with your child. Let rational thinking defuse the emotional intensity of prejudice.

At the same time, encourage positive values toward diversity and harmonious and cooperative ways of living. Love and respect your child so he or she can come to value and respect others.

. . . .

The Woman in a Wheelchair

Barry and Bobby were at the grocery store with their dad one day. They needed a few things for dinner and were helping their dad find the items in the store. When they turned down one of the aisles, they saw a woman in a wheelchair. She was trying to reach a jar of peanut butter on an upper shelf. Barry asked the woman if he could help her get the jar. The woman was very pleased to accept Barry's help and thanked him for being such a nice young man.

Later, in the car, Barry asked his dad why some of the customers in the store were staring at the woman in the wheelchair.

1. What do you suppose Barry and Bobby's dad said?
2. Do you know anyone who is confined to a wheel-chair? What are some of the challenges the person faces?
3. What do you think the boys learned from this incident?

. . . .

The Homeless

Abby missed the bus one day so her mom had to drive her to school. They were stopped for a red light at a busy intersection where many people were crossing the street. Abby noticed that several of these people looked somewhat shabby; their clothes were dirty and ragged. Some looked as if they just needed a good shower, and others were limping along slowly as if they were in pain. Abby asked her mother why those people looked the way they did.

Abby's mom said that some people have nowhere to live, so they live on the street or in cardboard houses (shacks) that they have made. That made Abby very sad.

1. How do homeless people stay warm in winter?

2. What do you know about shelters for homeless people?

3. Can you think of any ways you could help people who don't have homes?

. . . .

The Coat of Different Colors

The slamming of the front door announced that Jeremy was home from school. But one look at his frowning face told his mother he was not a happy camper. In answer to her question about how school had gone, he replied, "Terrible! That new kid in school—you know, the one I told you about who has that really weird-looking coat? Well, my teacher told me that I needed to be his buddy and show him around school, kind of get him used to everything and meet everyone."

This didn't seem to be a problem to Jeremy's mother, and she told him so. "But, Mother!" he exclaimed. "He looks so different with those funky clothes. Everyone will laugh at me if I start hanging around with him."

1. What would you say to Jeremy about spending time with the new boy?

2. Have you ever been afraid that someone would make fun of you because you spent time with someone who looked a little strange or wore clothes that were different from everyone else's?

3. Do you think Jesus chose his friends just because they wore the right clothes? What do you think he looked at when he chose his friends?

17

children with Disabilities

....

To the Parents

Much like the previous section, this section is about respecting others and appreciating and accepting their differences. Galatians 3:28 reminds us that we are all considered equal in the body of Christ: "There is neither Jew nor Greek, slave nor free, male nor female, for you are all one in Christ Jesus." We can keep that verse in mind as a guiding principle in teaching our children how to treat others.

It is a safe assumption that your children know someone with a disability. If your child has a sibling with a disability, you have probably already dealt with their feelings about it. However, if they have a schoolmate with a disability, they might not know how to bring it up or you might not know yourself. Some of the following stories should help to begin this very important dialogue.

Today's schools typically include children who have learning, emotional, and physical disabilities in the regular classroom. The children and their teachers receive help from specialized teachers and therapists. This extra assistance enables children with special needs to actively participate in a regular classroom. Also, this integration helps the other children in the class to realize that though others may look or act different, they can all learn from each other.

· · · · · · ·

Living with a Handicapped Sister

Seven-year-old Luis had a four-year-old sister, Marisa, who could not walk and had to be in a wheelchair. Because of her handicap, it took the family a long time to get into the car for church, shopping, or any other excursions. There were other inconveniences too. Luis had more responsibilities than some of his friends because his mother had to spend most of her time caring for little Marisa.

Sometimes Luis thought he wasn't getting the attention he deserved. He even felt angry at his little sister. This made him feel sad because he loved Marisa, but he just didn't know how to be mad and loving at the same time.

1. What kinds of responsibilities do you think Luis had?
2. How would you feel if you were in Luis's situation?
3. What should Luis do?

Problems with the New Baby

Brad and Cerise were excited to see their new baby brother, Anthony. Some of their friends had little sisters and brothers and they thought it was pretty cool.

The day after Anthony was born, Dad picked up Brad and Cerise from school and took them to the hospital to see him. On the way he explained that Anthony had been born too soon and had some breathing problems. Brad and Cerise were sad to hear that. When they saw their baby brother, they were surprised at how small he was.

After a few days, their mom came home from the hospital. Brad and Cerise had really missed her and couldn't wait to have their usual after-school talks. But it seemed she was always too tired to listen to them.

Baby Anthony finally came home from the hospital. Brad and Cerise were expecting a rosy-cheeked baby who smiled at them and slept a lot. Unfortunately, this baby cried all the time, and their mom and dad were always busy with him. This made Brad and Cerise feel left out.

1. Do you have a baby brother or sister who takes up a lot of your parents' time? How does that make you feel?
2. What could Brad and Cerise do to help with the new baby?

. . . .

Amy's New Friend

Amy was very excited when she came home from her first day at school. She immediately started telling her mother about Andrew, the new boy in her class. Amy told her mother that Andrew couldn't hear, but he had a woman with him who showed him hand signals to let him know what the teacher was saying. Amy asked her mother if she could learn some of those signals so that she could talk to Andrew too.

1. Do you know anyone with a hearing problem? What do you think it's like to be deaf?
2. What could Amy do to make Andrew feel welcome in his new class?
3. Do you think Amy would want to have Andrew for a friend? Why?

18

Doing and Saying the Right Thing

To the Parents

On a daily basis, we are confronted with the challenge of doing and saying the right thing. Do we shake our fist at the driver who beat us to our parking spot? Do we lose our temper with members of our family, friends, or strangers? Do we fudge a little bit with the ten items or less line at the grocery store? Do we tell a little white lie to get out of that dinner meeting with the boss?

While we may not think that our children notice when we skate over the edge of truthfulness, they are taking it all in, and they will remember. They will remember that it is sometimes okay to tell a little white lie if it makes their life more convenient. So, the next time you ask them to clean their room, they might tell you it is already clean. And the next time you ask them what they did at a friend's house, they might lie about the shows they watched and how they really spent their time.

The stories in this section are as much to remind you about the fine line of moral actions as they are to teach your child. Just remember, actions are more important than words.

·······

The "Yes" Girl

Tina had an older sister named Teresa. When Teresa's friends played at her house, Tina tried really hard to get them to notice her and include her in their activities. One way she did this was by agreeing with them on any subject they might be talking about, even if she didn't agree at all.

Tina also changed her ideas to fit the way that her own friends thought about things. This happened especially when the friend she was with became outspoken and extroverted in her opinions.

Tina's mom has noticed that Tina would change her story when she thinks it will help her become closer to a friend or fit in with an older crowd. Mom has told Tina that it is important for her to remain true to herself and that her friends will like her because of her honesty.

1. It is hard when you feel left out and really want to belong to a group. What are some ways that Tina might feel more comfortable expressing her own opinions?

2. If you were Tina's friend, what would you tell her about making and keeping friends?

3. Do you think people will like you because of your honesty?

. . . .

The Showoff

Greg was a friendly and happy five-year-old. He loved to play and wanted everyone around him to have fun too.

One day his parents had company over for a barbecue. Included in the group were three girls who were a little older than Greg, and he was delighted to be able to entertain them. They all had a good time playing with Greg's stuff, but after a while the girls decided to go outside and play on his "play structure." The three girls started ignoring Greg, so he tried to get their attention. First, he did his Tarzan yells. The girls just looked at him and went on with what they were doing.

So Greg went into the garage and got out his bike. The garage was up on a little hill, so Greg got to the highest spot, and without a helmet, gave himself a mighty push and went sailing down the hill. His front wheel hit a small rock and Greg went flying!

Greg ended up in the hospital with a broken arm and a slight concussion. Oh, no! What happened? Greg's parents were relieved that Greg was okay, but they also had some serious questions for him.

1. What questions do you think Greg's parents had for him?

2. What do you think made Greg want to show off?

3. Do you think Greg thought of the danger of riding his bike without a helmet and speeding down the driveway?

. . . .

The Giver

A trip to Target was one of Blair's all-time favorite activities. It was always a great time with her mom, and she loved the sheer number of possible items to buy. Almost every time she went, she was allowed to buy one little treat for herself. Sometimes it was a piece of candy, sometimes it was a little book, and sometimes it was a small toy. That one little treat always brightened her day.

Because Blair knew how much she loved picking out her treat, she figured that her friends probably also loved getting a treat. Blair was a generous girl, so she spent a lot of time trying to decide what little gifts she could get for her friends. Whenever one of her friends had a fight with another kid or received a reprimand from a teacher, Blair would try to figure out what kind of gift would be best to cheer up her friend.

Because Blair thought about gifts for herself and her friends so much, she sometimes forgot about doing homework and chores around the house. Her mom would remind her about doing these things. Finally, her mom had to sit Blair down and have a serious talk with her about how much she thought about treats.

1. What do you think Blair's mom said to her?
2. Do you think Blair's mom was unhappy because Blair was a giver or because she spent so much time thinking about gifts?

116

3. What other kinds of gifts could Blair give to her friends to cheer them up? Could those gifts include things like hugs, jokes, or just listening? These gifts are called "gifts from the heart." What are your "gifts from the heart"?
4. When do you feel the most cared for by your friends? Is it when they get you a gift or when they tell you good things and show you that they care?
5. Jesus gave you a special gift. Do you know what it is?

. . . .

When Adults Ignore the Rules

Jake went to his friend Jon's house to play one Saturday. All week long the two had talked about what they were going to do on this special day. They had mentioned climbing the old maple tree near Jon's house and maybe even building a tree house.

They were sitting on the back porch wondering what to do first when Jon's dad came outside and suggested they all go for a bike ride. The boys thought that was a great idea. Jon's dad had an extra bike for Jake, but when Jake asked for a helmet, Jon's dad said he didn't need to wear one because they wouldn't be going that far.

Jake's parents had a firm rule that he must never ride a bike without wearing a helmet. Jake didn't know what to do.

1. What would you do if this happened to you?
2. What do you think Jake should do?

3. When an adult tells you to do something that you know is not allowed, what can you say or do?

. . . .

The Birthday Party

Pamela had a lot of friends, so it wasn't too surprising when she received two invitations to birthday parties. Unfortunately, they were both for the same time on the same day. One of the parties was going to be at a ranch, and the girls were going to ride horses. It was being given for Melissa, the most popular girl at school.

The other invitation was from Anna, Pamela's next-door neighbor. The two girls had been best friends for years and played together every day. Anna was inviting just a few friends to her house for a hot dog roast.

Pamela really wanted to go to Melissa's party; it sounded like a lot of fun! She was trying to figure out how she could sneak out of her house the day of the party so Anna wouldn't see her.

1. Have you ever been in a situation like this? What did you do?
2. What do you think Pamela should do?
3. How do you think Anna would feel if she saw Pamela sneaking out of her house?

. . . .

The Television Show

Joshua loved playing with his friend Aaron. They had been friends since preschool, and now they were already in the second grade. Joshua especially loved going to Aaron's house because Aaron's mom didn't have a lot of rules. She seemed more interested in letting the boys have fun.

One afternoon when Joshua was at Aaron's house, Aaron's mom turned on a television program that Joshua wasn't allowed to watch when he was at home. Joshua squirmed. His mom was very careful about what television shows she allowed him to watch. She always told him that violent scenes would get into his mind and he'd have a hard time forgetting them. Joshua didn't know what to do. He thought, *Should I tell Aaron's mom that I'm not allowed to watch this program or should I watch the show just this once?*

1. What might Aaron think of Joshua if he says he isn't allowed to watch this program?
2. Should Aaron's mom have asked Joshua if he was allowed to watch this program?
3. What would you do if you were Joshua?

19

Beat the clock

....

To the Parents

It seems that beating the clock is one of our society's biggest challenges. There are just not enough hours in the day to accomplish all that we need and want to do. Just think about the things parents do during an average day: fix breakfast, get kids dressed, pack lunches, make beds, take kids to school, go to work (in or outside the home), pick up kids from school, take kids to various activities, prepare dinner, wash dishes, do laundry, help kids with homework, prepare for the next day's activities, go through kids' nighttime routine, have quality time with spouse, and try to fit in at least a few minutes of relaxation. Consider that this list is just a bare-bones day; special events add even more challenges!

The key to handling all this comes from Proverbs 3:6 (NLT), which tells us, "Seek his [God's] will in all you do, and he will direct your paths." If you look at your schedule with an attitude of first seeking God's will, you can't help but alter your schedule dramatically. Our family struggles constantly to practice what we preach in this area. Prioritizing our lives and those of our children has been a guiding light for Geno and myself. Although we are often tempted to tack on another activity or two, we try to remember our commitment to control our schedule instead of letting it control us.

·······

Sally's Schedule

Sally was a very active ten-year-old. She knew that her mom loved her and was proud of everything she did at school and in music and sports. To please her mom, Sally went along with all the things her mom had added to her already busy schedule. However, by the end of the week, after piano lessons, dance class, karate, soccer, and schoolwork, Sally ended up feeling exhausted. She knew that she had opportunities her mom didn't have when she was Sally's age, but Sally didn't like being so busy. She hardly had time to play with her friends.

1. Why do you think Sally's mom wants Sally to be involved in so many activities?
2. What could Sally say to her mom to make her understand how she feels?

Derek the Dynamo

Twelve-year-old Derek loved sports. He played soccer, basketball, football—you name it, he wanted to play it! Derek's parents seemed to enjoy having him involved in sports just as much as he liked playing them. They were always on the sidelines cheering him on. They signed him up for the teams, took him to practices, washed his uniforms, and even kept score at the games.

There was only one problem. Before Derek started playing on so many teams, he and his family had attended church every Sunday. They were involved in Bible studies, attended summer camps, and had nightly devotions. Now their only devotions were short prayers before dinner, and they rarely made it to church or Bible studies. The more Derek thought about it, the more he wondered if he and his family were spending too much time with sports.

1. How could Derek and his parents get back to attending church and reading the Bible?
2. Is there some way Derek could play sports and still have time for church activities?

20

Faith and Spirituality

....

To the Parents

Children learn to pray with their parents at meals, at bedtime, and at church. But do children know why they pray? Here are some questions to ask yourself concerning your children's understanding of prayer.

- What are they praying for? Things, people, guidance?
- Do they expect prayer to be answered as requested?
- When they pray to Jesus for answers, do they expect Jesus to solve the dilemma for them without any effort on their part?

When you get into a dialogue about prayer with your children, the discussion may take some unexpected turns.

Try to keep your children on track while allowing them to express themselves.

As with prayer, it is important for children to see the connection between faith and everyday life. Throughout this book we have included some discussion questions that reflect on what Jesus would want children to do or think about. We encourage you to do the same throughout the day—simply talk about or ask what Jesus would want us to do in a particular situation. It is natural for Christians to ask Jesus to accompany us throughout our day, but children don't always know that this is an active process.

We teach children Bible verses and read them stories in the hope that the exercise will transfer in their thinking to the application of the principles. Parents have a very important assignment here: We must ensure that our children can make the transition. We must teach them how to do it, or it will be left to others.

. . . .

An Example for Jesus

Caleb and Eric were best friends. They went to each other's houses after school and played soccer together on Saturdays; the only day of the week that they *didn't* spend together was Sunday. On that day, Caleb went to church with his family, and Eric stayed home with his family. You see, Caleb's parents were Christians, but Eric's parents didn't believe in God.

Caleb knew that Jesus was in his heart and wished that Eric could also know Jesus. He had invited Eric to several youth events at his church, and Eric always had a great time. Eric had also learned how to pray and had asked his parents to take him to church on Sundays, but it seemed they always had other things to do.

1. Caleb really wanted Eric to ask Jesus into his heart, but he wasn't sure how to help that happen. How do you think he could talk to Eric about his faith?
2. Should Caleb pray that Eric and his family accept Jesus as their Lord and Savior? Can you think of what he might say while praying?
3. Would it be better for Caleb to show by his actions and behaviors that he is a Christian or by just telling Caleb about being a Christian? Which do you think would be more convincing to Caleb?

. . . .

The Children Who Lived in the Dump

A kindergarten teacher at a Christian school noticed that the children in her class always prayed for things they wanted, like the latest toys and clothes. Troubled by this trend, she told them a true story about the children who live in the Payatas dump in Manila, Philippines. These children scavenge their food and clothing from a trash heap.

Feeling sorry for the children in the Philippines, the kindergarteners began holding bake sales to raise money. The five-year-olds also filled gift boxes for the children in the dump. One child brought a shoebox filled with soap, toothbrushes, and toothpaste. Another child brought a box that had a pair of slippers and some small toys in it.

1. What could you do to help needy children?
2. How does it make you feel when you hear that some children are still hungry when they go to bed?

·······

The Good Friday Question

On Good Friday, eight-year-old Ethan went to church with his family. After the service was over, Ethan's younger brothers, Mitchell and Robert, had a lot of questions about the meaning of Good Friday.

On the way home, they asked their mom and dad why Jesus had died on the cross. As they were trying to figure out how to turn an adult-sized answer into a child-sized one, Ethan spoke up. He said, "I know why Jesus died on the cross for us!" He did it so he could provide a bridge from earth to heaven where God lives. There is no sin in heaven so we had to have a way to get there, because all of us on earth have sinned."

1. Why do you think Jesus died for us?
2. How would you explain Jesus' dying on the cross to someone who didn't know anything about it?

21

Standing Up for Yourself and Others

....

To the Parents

Have you heard of bully-proofing? It seems that in some neighborhoods and schools, kids are showing other kids how to play nicely. Kids are given effective "talking tools" to use with bullies. For example, if these children see someone bullying another child, they try to stop the bully by saying, "We don't talk like that to other kids, and if you keep teasing, we won't be able to play with you."

If the bully persists, an adult is called over and told about it. The adult may then remove the bully until he or she decides others should not be teased or bullied. The adult makes it clear to the child that this kind of behavior is wrong and that it will keep them from making friends.

Bullying is a common thread among children who do not know positive ways of interacting with others, whether it is due to childhood abuse, neglect, or some other negative influence. Moreover, bullying is clearly involved in the development of a wide range of major childhood adjustment problems, including failure in school and rejection by peers. There is even a growing body of evidence that suggests that hard-to-manage preschoolers are at high risk for clinically significant problems in later childhood.

When the negative behavior is stopped and the bully learns new and better behaviors, he or she has a better chance to make friends and to be more successful in school. The children who help the bully also learn that caring for others involves having the courage to put a stop to hurtful behaviors.

·······

The Guilt Giver

Keith and Cody were in the same class at school and often played together. They were both smart boys, but Cody was learning some unfortunate tricks. He knew how to take advantage of Keith. One day, when he was at Keith's house, he noticed that Keith had a new toy robot. Cody had been wanting one for a long time. He knew that if he cried and told a sad story about never getting any new toys, Keith was likely to feel sorry for him and give him *his* robot.

On this day, however, Keith stood his ground and told Cody he couldn't have the robot. Well, Cody pitched a huge fit! Keith decided that he really didn't know how to handle this situation without some help, so he asked his mother what he should do. Keith's mom told him that he did not have to give Cody the robot and Cody's mom could settle things when she arrived to pick him up. Keith's mom also told him that he had done the right thing and gave him a hug for standing up for himself.

1. What do you think Cody's mom might say to him when she finds out that he tried to take Keith's robot?
2. Do you think Keith did the right thing? Do you think he should have done something else?
3. It is hard to deal with friends when they try to make you feel guilty so that you do something you don't want to do. What are some things you can say when that happens?

· · · · · · ·

Dealing with the Mean Kid

Carly's mom and dad taught her to be kind to others. And most of the time she was adorable! Everyone remarked about how agreeable she was.

When Carly went to kindergarten, she met a whole new set of people. One of the girls in the class pinched and pushed Carly. Carly didn't know what to do. Kindness had always worked out for her, but she didn't know if it would work on this girl.

After Carly was in bed one night, her dad came to tuck her in and asked about her day. Carly told him about the girl at school and that she almost felt like being mean back.

Carly's dad thought for a moment, then said, "I wonder if you should talk to her about the problem. You could tell her that you'd like to be her friend, but you can't if she's going to be so mean and hurtful. I'm sure she'll listen to you"

The next night Carly's dad asked her how her school day had gone. "Great, Dad," she said. "You were right. I talked to the mean girl and she listened to what I said. She wants to be friends!"

1. What did Carly learn from this problem?
2. What if Carly had just been mean back to the girl?

· · · · · · ·

The Teaser

Damian's mother had brought him to the park. As she watched him play on the merry-go-round, she overheard him talking to an older boy who had been teasing other kids. Damian's mother smiled when she heard Damian say to the older boy, "My mom said that it is not okay to use words like that and to tease other kids. If you don't stop teasing them, we won't play with you anymore."

1. What would you have done if you were Damian?
2. Why do you think some children tease or bully others?

Gary and the Girl

One day Gary was playing tag with his buddies, Colin and Mike, on the playground. Takeshia, one of the girls in their third-grade class, asked if she could join them. In a mean voice Colin said to her, "No way! We don't let girls play this game." Takeshia looked as if she was about to cry but tried one more time to join in. This time Colin made a face at her and said, "No girls allowed." When Takeshia started to walk away, Gary went after her. "I'll play with you," he said.

1. How does this story show the difference between talking brave and actually being brave?
2. Do you think Gary should have told Colin and Mike that they weren't being very nice to Takeshia? Why, or why not?
3. Can you think of a time when you did the right thing even if it wasn't what your friends were doing?

22

Helping Others

....

To the Parents

Compassion is often thought of simply as an attitude of the heart, as in "She has such compassion for others." However, it is both an emotion and an action. As people of moral and ethical character, we are called to be moved by the needs and hurts of those around us. It is easy to recognize the face of compassion. We see it in people who faithfully work in soup kitchens, underpaid teachers who work with disadvantaged children, and overworked but committed social workers.

We also see compassion in smaller but no less important actions. We find it in friends who prepare meals for new mothers, friends who show up to hold the hand of someone with a spouse having surgery, friends who lovingly yet firmly confront someone about a substance abuse problem, and friends who listen, comfort, and don't judge.

Having a compassionate friend results in treasures and gifts that are unimaginable, but being a compassionate friend can bring even greater rewards. We hope that these stories will help build and strengthen the compassion that rests in your child's heart.

. . . .

The Stepmother

Boyd's parents were divorced when he was four. Now his father had remarried, and although his new stepmother seemed nice, things had gotten complicated. One of the biggest things was that his father wanted to do everything with *her* and they never went anywhere without *her*. Boyd and his father used to do dad-son things, but now his stepmother always had to be included. Boyd missed that one-on-one time with his father. He also wished that his stepmother would go away so that his parents could get back together and they could be a family again, even though his mother had told him that she and his dad would never remarry.

Boyd also had some other questions about his new stepmother. For instance, what should he call her? Boyd didn't want to call her "mom" because he already had a mom. He also wondered about whether or not he had to do what his stepmother told him to do. She wasn't his mom or his teacher. When he was at his dad's house, he had to obey a different set of rules than at his house with his mom, and it was confusing to remember which rules went where.

1. Who can answer all of Boyd's questions?
2. How could Boyd tell his father that he would like to spend some more time doing dad-son things?
3. What would you tell Boyd about finding answers to his questions about how he should act with his stepmother?
4. What could Boyd do to have a closer relationship with his stepmother?
5. How should Boyd find out what to call his step-mother?

. . . .

Helping the Homeless

Colleen's mom belonged to a group of women who liked to help others in their community. One of their missions was cooking and taking food to people at a homeless shelter. Colleen had promised to help her mom every Wednesday after school for a whole year.

At first Colleen enjoyed talking with the people and helping out at the shelter. After a few months, however, Colleen decided she'd rather spend Wednesday after-noons with her friends. She didn't understand why her mom was so upset about her decision.

1. Colleen promised her mother that she would help her for the whole year. Can she back out without breaking her promise?

STORIES

2. What is Colleen learning by helping her mother feed the homeless?

3. In the Bible we read about Jesus feeding people. What do these stories teach us?

. . . .

Monsters in the Night

Debbie, Kelsey, and Emily were spending the night at their friend Samantha's house. The girls were sound asleep when Debbie suddenly started crying in her sleep. The other girls woke up, turned on the light, and crept over to Debbie's sleeping bag. After they gently shook her awake, Debbie told them she had been having a nightmare about monsters chasing her. She said the dream had frightened her because it seemed so real. The other girls put their arms around Debbie and told her they would keep the light on until she went back to sleep.

1. What if the other girls had laughed at Debbie?

2. How did Kelsey, Emily, and Samantha show compassion?

3. Can you think of a time when someone showed compassion to you?

23

Happy to Be Me

....

To the Parents

My son Austin loves to look at himself in the mirror. We mounted a kid-level mirror on the side of a dresser in his room so he can examine his reflection whenever he feels the need. Sometimes he inspects a scratch or a cut; sometimes he checks out a new outfit. He also looks in the mirror when he is trying a new expression, such as just the right scary face. Whatever the reason, it comes down to the same need—to obtain affirmation of who he is to others and to himself. He needs to know how he appears to others, and by looking in the mirror he can find out.

This desire to have someone reflect us in an accepting way is a universal need. Children look to their parents to provide this kind of affirmation for them. They are constantly growing and learning and therefore need to have their new selves reflected accurately by those they trust the most. If parents do this well, children will feel more secure and ready to face the outside world.

·······

The Adopted Boy

Nathan's mom was very young when he was born. Although she loved him, she knew she wouldn't be able to take good care of him as he grew up. Because of this, she found a family that really wanted another child and would be able to give him a good home. So, soon after Nathan was born, he was adopted by Mr. and Mrs. Clement, who already had two children—Elliott and Hannah. They happily welcomed the new baby into their family.

When Nathan was old enough to understand, his parents told him about how much his mom had loved him and how brave she was to let him grow up in a good home. They made sure he knew how much they loved him, because to them he was just the same as their other two children.

As Nathan grew older, he started to notice how different he was from his brother and sister. He didn't like it whenever Elliott would say, "I have Daddy's eyes." Nathan couldn't say that because he didn't know what *his* daddy's eyes looked like. His very worst thought was that maybe his mother really didn't want him and that was the reason she gave him up to be adopted. He hated being different.

1. Whom should Nathan talk to about his feelings?
2. If you were adopted, do you think you'd feel any different about your family than you do right now?
3. How would you make Nathan feel better about being adopted?

· · · · · · · ·

Feeling Blue

Sometimes, for no particular reason, Elisabeth had a *bad* day. She'd wake up just not feeling right, drag herself out of bed, get dressed, eat breakfast, and trudge off to school. It seemed like once a bad day began, there was nothing Elisabeth could do to make it go right.

On other days, Elisabeth jumped out of bed, wore one of her favorite outfits, ate her favorite breakfast, and bounced off to school. On these days, she did great in class, everyone liked her, and she just smiled all day!

These changes in feelings were very confusing to Elisabeth because she really wanted every day to be a good day. She wondered how she could make every day be a good one.

1. What makes the beginning to a good day?
2. What makes the beginning to a *bad* day?
3. How can Elisabeth change a bad day into a good day?
4. Have you ever been able to change a bad day into a good day?

5. Have you ever had a good day turn bad? How?

....

The Tiniest Girl

Mei Lin was very small for her age. Even though she was in the second grade, people were always asking her if she went to school yet. That embarrassed her. She couldn't understand why people would say such things.

At school, Mei Lin's friends tended to try to take care of her because they thought of her as being weak. Whenever they played house, they wanted her to be the baby.

Mei Lin hated being so small. Her parents always said they liked her the way she was, but she didn't know if she believed them.

1. What could Mei Lin say to people who ask her if she is old enough for school?
2. Would you like to be smaller or bigger than you are? How would your life be different if you were?
3. What else could Mei Lin's parents do or say to make her feel better about herself?

....

The Princess Girl

Janie lived in a nice house; at least she thought it was nice until she went to Ashley's house one day after school. Ashley and her family lived in a huge, fancy house. Her mom bought Ashley all the clothes and toys she wanted and had Ashley's room decorated so it looked like a castle for a fairy princess. It seemed like a dream come true to Janie.

When Janie went back home that day, her own house seemed somehow smaller and uglier than it had been that morning. *I'd be embarrassed to have Ashley come here,* thought Janie. She knew she'd never have all the things Ashley had.

As they spent more time together, Janie saw that she and Ashley lived very different lives. Ashley's family didn't believe in Jesus, so they didn't go to church or pray together like Janie's family did. Ashley's parents let Ashley make her own choices about what television shows she wanted to watch, but Ashley made choices that seemed all wrong to Janie. Sometimes, after spending time with Ashley, Janie just wanted to go back home where things felt safe.

1 Who would you rather be—Janie or Ashley? Why?
2. What does "the grass is always greener on the other side of the fence" mean?
3. What does it mean to be grateful? What did Janie have to be grateful for?

. . . .

Luke, the Lanky Boy

Luke had always been thin. He didn't mind that too much, but during the summer between third and fourth grade, he grew three inches. Then he *really* looked skinny.

Bryce, one of the older boys at school, made fun of Luke every day at recess; he laughed at him and called him names like "weakling" and "scarecrow-boy." Luke

143

wanted to get along with the other kids at his school. Bryce had really hurt Luke's feelings, and Luke didn't know what to do. Luke was tired of being teased, and he wished he wasn't so tall and thin. *Why can't I just look like the other kids?* he thought.

1. What do you think Luke should do?
2. Have you ever felt like someone was criticizing you for the way you looked? What did you do? How did you feel about it?
3. How do you and your friends talk about someone who looks different? Do you make fun of them behind their back or even directly to them?

········

Lonely in the First Grade

One day at school, Sarah was feeling very lonely. She was the last one chosen for the games on the playground, and it seemed that no one wanted to sit with her at lunchtime. She decided it was because her new glasses made her double ugly and no one would ever like her.

When Sarah got home from school that day, she told her mother she hated school and didn't want to go anymore. "How come no one else in the whole first grade has to wear glasses?" she asked with tears streaming down her cheeks.

1. What could Sarah's mother say to make her feel better?
2. Can you think of a time when you felt like Sarah did?
3. What should Sarah do?

HAPPY TO BE ME

The Child of Divorce

When Blaine was three, his mother and father divorced. His father married another woman and moved away. Blaine didn't get to see his father very often. He loved his mom a lot, but she just didn't know how to do dad-type things. She was always tired because she had to work so hard. When Blaine visited friends from his fourth-grade class, he noticed that their dads played ball with them, helped them build cars, and taught them how to fish.

Blaine felt as if he was really different from his friends; he thought no one understood him. He felt angry too, because he was missing out on special father-son stuff. He wondered if maybe it was *his* fault that his parents divorced. Maybe he wasn't a good baby or child and that was why his father left them.

1. Blaine had many painful questions that needed to be answered. Where do you think he could go to find some of the answers?
2. Is it okay to feel angry sometimes? Why, or why not?
4. How would you let Blaine know that it was not his fault his parents were divorced?

24

Too Much Can Be Way Too Much

....

To the Parents

Graysen is a materially minded boy. He loves his toys and possessions and is always thinking about how to obtain more. Dealing with his constant quest for attainment can be challenging, but he does have a saving grace. He has a generous heart and truly and sincerely cares for others. For instance, if he gets a sticker or toy from the dentist, he always asks for one for each of his brothers.

We use Graysen's compassionate nature to help him tone down his desire to acquire. Our talks with him often revolve around giving to others. These stories hit their mark. The compassionate nature that he was given pulls him out of the selfish nature that is spurred on by skillful marketing techniques. He still struggles and probably always will, but our stories open an important dialogue with him about selfishness versus selflessness.

Just recently, Graysen opted to pull money out of his own piggy bank to give to the charity that was being hosted by his Vacation Bible School. This was of his own volition, even after we had extended the money for his offering. As parents, all we could do was smile!

. . . .

I Scream for Ice Cream!

Like a lot of little girls (and boys), Lisa loved ice cream: vanilla, chocolate, chocolate chip, strawberry—you name it, she loved it. Her parents let her have ice cream after dinner, but they always limited it to just one scoop. She hated having only one scoop and dreamed of the day when she could eat all the ice cream she wanted.

One night when her grandmother was babysitting her, Lisa's dream came true. After dinner, when her grandmother asked if she wanted a little treat, Lisa replied that she would like some ice cream. She fibbed and said her mom and dad always let her scoop out her own. While her grandmother was in the living room, Lisa filled a big soup bowl with ice cream. When she finished that, she refilled her bowl again and again until the ice cream was gone. For the first time, Lisa had eaten all the ice cream she wanted.

At first Lisa was happy and content, but soon she started feeling really full, then really uncomfortable, and then really sick! The worst part was that she had to tell her parents the truth when they came home.

1. Why did Lisa's parents let her have just one scoop of ice cream after dinner?
2. What does the word *moderation* mean?
3. Is there something in your life that you love more than anything else? What would you do to get it? If you had too much of it, what might happen?

· · · · · · ·

The New Stuff

Courtney noticed that Danielle, another girl in her class, always had something new to wear. It seemed to Courtney that Danielle had a new outfit just about every week. Courtney began to look at what was in her own closet, and she was not pleased.

One day after school, Courtney decided to talk to her mother about buying some new clothes. "Please can we go shopping?" she begged. "I don't have anything to wear."

"Courtney Lynne, you have a closet full of clothes!" said her mother.

"Mom, all my stuff is old! The other kids won't like me unless I have new outfits like Danielle's."

1. What do you think Courtney's mother should say?
2. Courtney says that kids won't like her unless she gets new outfits. Do you think that's true?
3. Do you think Danielle was happy just because she got new things all the time? Why, or why not?

Meltdown in the Market

One day Gabriel was shopping with his mother in the supermarket. As they were checking out, he saw a little girl who was dressed up like a princess. She was wearing a frilly dress and party shoes and had a tiara perched on her blond head. She certainly wasn't acting like a princess, though! This little girl was yelling, and she kicked at her mother with all her might.

Everyone in the checkout lanes turned to look at the little girl, who was now screaming, "I want more candy! I want more! Right now, Mommy!" Gabriel could see that she already had a candy bar in her hand, but apparently it wasn't enough for her. Then Gabriel saw the girl's mother reach for another candy bar and hand it to her.

1. What made the little girl's mother give her another candy bar?
2. What do you think the mother should have done?
3. What do you think will happen the next time the little girl goes to the grocery store with her mother?

25

Do Your Best

....

To the Parents

When I was young, I showed horses competitively. As my skills improved and I won more classes, my desire to win also increased. This feeling of competitiveness pervaded everything in my life, even my relationships with my peers. For example, my poor prom date drove four hours to pick me up from a horse show and take me to the dance (yes, I showered before going!). Afterwards, he drove me back so that I could show the next day. I couldn't even put off one day of showing to go to the biggest social event of my high school career!

Because my constant focus on winning resulted in much success, I was rewarded for this behavior. It was only later as an adult that I began to have some perspective on my past behavior and attitudes. It was only with the grace of God and fellowship with good friends that I learned how to put competition into proper perspective.

Today, as I watch my sons begin their forays into the world of competition, I am torn with how best to guide them. The old part of me wants to emphasize that "winning isn't everything; it's the only thing!" The more nurturing mother in me, however, encourages them to simply do their best while having a healthy sense of empathy for their friends and companions.

. . . .

Play Fair

Colin and Robby burst through the back door after soccer practice and started telling their mom about Chip, another boy on their team. Colin told his mom he was miffed because Chip had knocked him down to get to the ball. "It makes me want to knock him down and kick him!" he said.

"Me, too," said Robby, since Chip had knocked him down too. Their mom then asked about how Chip played.

"Oh, he's our best player!" said Colin.

"And he gets more points than anyone!" added Robby.

"So, can you think of some ways to deal with this?" their mom asked. "Violence isn't the answer, you know."

1. Can you think of some solutions to Colin and Robby's problem?
2. What do you think could be the real reason Colin and Robby are upset with Chip?

Tracey Blows Her Own Horn

Tracey loved to ride and show her horse, Sundance. She rode and had lessons from her trainer almost every day of the week. Because she practiced so much, she became a very good rider, winning ribbons and trophies whenever she went to horse shows. Her best friend, Alyssa, also showed horses; the girls got along well even though sometimes one or the other would win a particular class.

After some time, Tracey started to win the jumping class show after show. Her winning started to make her feel overconfident, and one day before a class she boasted to Alyssa, "I'll bet I'm going to win this class again!" Alyssa, shocked and a little angry at Tracey's claim, promised herself that she was going to do everything she could to beat Tracey!

1. What do you think would happen to Tracey and Alyssa's friendship after this?
2. When Tracey realizes that she was being rude, how should she make it up to her friend?
3. How do you feel about competing with your friends? How do you manage to stay friends with them after you have competed? Is it ever okay to lose just so that your friends won't get mad at you?

. . . .

The Best Reader

Juan and Travis were best friends in first grade. They loved to play together and even got to sit next to each other in class. They both worked hard on their class work and always got along well. However, one day after reading time, Travis told Juan that he was a better reader than Juan. Juan was hurt and discouraged but didn't say anything to Travis.

Later that afternoon Juan told his mom what had happened. She told him Travis wasn't being a good friend when he said that, and Juan should tell him how he was feeling. She also told Juan that he needed to concentrate only on his own reading and not compare himself to anyone else. She told Juan that he was improving in his ability to read and she was very proud of him for doing his best.

1. Have you ever been told by a friend that you didn't do something as well as they did? How did you feel when your friend said this?
2. What did you say back to your friend?
3. Why is it important not to compare yourself to others?

. . . .

Deborah versus the Piano

Deborah was jealous. Her best friend, Ella, could play the piano and sometimes played solos in church. Deborah begged and pleaded with her mother and father to let her take piano lessons. Finally her parents agreed and found a teacher for her.

Much to Deborah's surprise, she found out that it was *hard* to play the piano. Not only did she have to learn the notes, she had to practice every day! And even after all that work, sometimes the songs still didn't sound right.

After only three months of lessons, Deborah had had enough, and she told her parents she wanted to quit. To her surprise, they told her she couldn't.

1. Were Deborah's parents just being mean or did they want her to learn something? What could she learn by sticking with the lessons?
2. Have you ever wanted to quit something once you started it? What happened?
3. What does *self-discipline* mean?

. . . .

Race Car Mania

Every Friday night, Peter attended a kids' club at his church. The group was made up of kids of all ages, and they had fun singing, playing games, and learning about Jesus. One week, the leader announced that there was going to be a race car contest. He said everyone could buy a kit for $5.00 and build their very own toy race car. They could decorate it any way they wanted and enter it in the contest the next Friday evening.

Peter and his father spent an afternoon putting together a car. They sanded it, painted it, and even put some cool stickers on it. The night of the contest, Peter and his father arrived at the church. Peter looked around at the other kids' cars. Many of them looked much fancier than his; some even had spoilers and special wheels. When Peter saw the trophies for the best race cars, his heart started to beat faster. He wanted one of those!

Everyone was quiet as the leader announced the winners. Peter was given a ribbon for participating, but the trophies went to the boys who had added special options to their cars. He was very disappointed. He didn't even want to stay for refreshments. All he wanted to do was go home, throw away his car, and forget about the contest.

1. What should Peter's father say to him?
2. Whose fault was it that Peter lost the contest?
3. Was Peter being a poor loser? Have you ever been a poor loser? When?

. . . .

Melissa and the Writing Contest

Merrick excelled at everything. He got good grades, was very athletic, had lots of friends, and was involved in many school activities. With all of his activities, he brought home many prizes and rewards. He was the center of attention. His sister, Melissa, was rather shy but didn't mind being in the background.

One day Melissa heard about a writing contest with a first prize of $100 for the best story. Melissa loved to write, and she wrote a story about flying around—just floating anywhere and everywhere. To her surprise, and everyone else's, Melissa won the contest. She was so excited!

Although her parents were excited about Melissa winning the contest and made a big deal about it, Merrick didn't know how to react. He was used to being the one who stood out, and he didn't know what to think about all the attention being paid to Melissa.

1. Why do you think Merrick wasn't very enthusiastic about Melissa winning the prize?
2. Do you think that winning the contest might change the way Merrick and Melissa get along with each other?
3. Do you think this might change the way Melissa feels about herself? Could it take away some of her shyness?

26

Safety

....

To the Parents

It seems that children want out of their strollers too soon! Safety issues become very apparent when we cannot keep toddlers in one place while another child needs our full attention. Children are adept at getting lost in a split second. So it becomes job number one to teach children what to do when they are lost or when someone they don't know tries to talk to them.

Children should be taught their phone numbers, addresses, and full names at a young age and taught to look for an appropriate adult if they are lost or confused. Finding a mother with her children is usually a safe bet for

159

them. If children are lost in a store or shopping mall, they can go to the information desk or look for a uniformed employee.

Water safety is another huge issue. Since water is a source of so much fun, it is hard for a child to realize that it is also a place of danger. A very dangerous point in an early swimmer's awareness of the water is when he or she has just made a breakthrough in swimming lessons. The child may become overconfident and assume it is okay to swim without an adult.

In the southwest city where I (Pat) spend a great deal of the year, drowning deaths and near deaths are reported daily. Children can drown in even a small amount of water, such as in a bathtub or a large pail. Wherever there is water, adults must watch small children closely.

· · · · · · ·

A Day at the Beach

Four-year-old Steven loved taking swimming lessons. He thought he was hot stuff in the water. Whenever he jumped into the pool, he could paddle straight ahead to the safety of the side. Steven was sure he was a good swimmer.

One beautiful summer day, Steven's family went to the beach. The water was warm, and Steven wanted to try out his new swimming skills. He begged his mom and dad to let him swim without his lifejacket; they said he could, but just for a few minutes.

Steven had gone a few feet from shore when a big wave came rolling in and knocked him in the water face first. Steven tried to swim, but he didn't know which way to go and actually started swimming farther out. Suddenly, two big hands grabbed Steven and pulled him to safety. Dad was there to save him.

1. Was Steven overconfident about water? After all, he had taken lessons. Shouldn't that be enough?
2. What did Steven learn about water that he did not know before?

. . . .

Remembering the Rules

One morning on their way to school, Joan and Jeremy were going to meet their friend Amanda just up the block. They were about a half block from Amanda when they saw a car stop and the driver motion for Amanda to get into the car. Joan and Jeremy started yelling and running toward Amanda. Just then the car sped off.

When they reached Amanda, Joan and Jeremy were out of breath; they told her they needed to hurry to school to tell the principal what had happened. "Why?" said Amanda. "That man just wanted me to help him find his lost puppy."

"I can't believe it!" said Joan. "Don't you remember the safety rules we learned from that policeman in our assembly?"

"Sure, but this was different—that man needed my help!" Amanda said.

As they hurried to school, Joan and Jeremy reviewed with Amanda the safety rules they had learned:

If a stranger in a car approaches you, run away; tell your parents or teachers about it.

161

Never speak to people you don't know unless you are with a family member.

If someone is following you, run to the nearest house.

Tell authorities immediately if someone you don't know asks to take pictures of you.

If at all possible, don't go anywhere alone.

1. What should you do if you are late and someone you don't know offers you a ride? What if the parent of one of your friends offers you a ride?

2. If an adult you don't know asks you something, is it rude to just not answer? What should you do?

3. What would you do if someone you didn't know told you that your mother had sent him or her to pick you up at school?

. . . .

Morning at the Mall

Seven-year-old Ben and his five-year-old twin brothers were excited about the new school year. One Saturday morning their mom decided they should go to the mall to buy new school shoes.

When they got to the shoe store, it was very busy, and they had to sit and wait for a few minutes (to the twins it felt like an hour!). Finally, the clerk came to help the boys try on and select shoes.

The boys' mom asked Ben to keep an eye on his brothers while she went to the counter to pay for the shoes. When Ben wasn't looking, the twins walked out of the store. They headed for the merry-go-round in the middle of the mall and stood there watching it go around and

ر

around. After a few minutes, they decided to go back to the shoe store, but they couldn't remember which way to go. They were frightened.

1. What should the twins do now?
2. Was it a good idea for the boys' mom to ask Ben to keep an eye on his brothers? Why, or why not?
3. Have you ever been lost? What did you do?
4. Even though there were two of them, what made this an unsafe activity?
5. How can they get help?
6. Would it be a good idea to go in different directions?

27

Holidays

....

To the Parents

Many holidays skip by us without much recognition except for our enjoying a three- or four-day weekend. The major holidays such as Thanksgiving and Christmas have traditions surrounding them, but what about holidays like Labor Day and Presidents' Day? These special days are prime opportunities for teaching our children about qualities of character. As you will see, many of the stories behind holidays are intriguing and filled with adventure and drama. If we simply view holidays as a break from the routine of daily life, we are missing valuable object lessons that will help develop our children's character.

New Year's Day

January 1, New Year's Day, is known as a day of reflection and planning for the future. Reflection means looking back at what has happened and where we have been. When we look back, we see things about ourselves we'd like to change, and when we look ahead, we think about ways to make those changes. These plans for the future are called New Year's resolutions.

Because we don't often have time for really thinking about our lives, the first day of each year is a good time to do just that.

1. Do you know why most of the stores are closed and there is no mail today?
2. What do you think the word *reflection* means? How about *resolution?*
3. Can you think of some resolutions? Let me share one of mine for this year.

• • • • • • •

Valentine's Day

One of the legends about Valentine's Day involves Saint Valentine, a priest from Rome. Emperor Claudius decided that single men made better soldiers than those with wives and families. As a result, he outlawed marriage for young men. Valentine knew that this was unfair, so he continued to perform marriages in secret. Valentine's actions were eventually discovered, however, and he was arrested and later died on February 14. This is how February 14 came to be known as Valentine's Day. We celebrate love on this day because Valentine dared to risk his own life for the sake of love.

1. Do you know someone who gave his life just because of his love for you?
2. How do you show your love for others on Valentine's Day? How is that different than how you show them love on other days?

. . . .

Presidents' Day

Presidents' Day takes place in February, when we observe the birthdays of Abraham Lincoln and George Washington. Abraham Lincoln was a great president of the United States. He loved our country and felt that slavery was wrong. He tried to abolish (get rid of) slavery, but the people in the South who owned slaves did not want to give them up. The slaveholders thought they were necessary for harvesting cotton and other crops, but the people in the northern states wanted the slaves to be freed. The Northerners and the Southerners could not agree, and so they went to war. The war was called the Civil War. Many young men were killed, and eventually slavery was abolished.

George Washington was a leader of the American Revolution. The American Revolution happened because Americans wanted to become independent from Britain— Americans wanted to have their own government instead of having Britain rule them. George Washington led the armies that won independence from the British.

After the American Revolution, George Washington was elected as the first president of the United States. He and the Congress created a brand-new government for the United States of America. Many cities, streets, and schools (and even a state) are named for him.

1. What do you know about Abraham Lincoln? Do you know his nickname?
2. What do you think about slavery?
3. What do you think that George Washington did that was important enough to have a special day and so many things named after him?
4. What do you think made people choose George Washington as their first president? How do you think people chose a leader in those days?

• • • • • • •

Saint Patrick's Day

Saint Patrick was born in England. When he was sixteen he was captured by Irish raiders and forced into slavery in Ireland. He was unhappy and prayed to God constantly. His prayers were answered after six years, and he was sent back to England.

After he became a priest in England, he returned to Ireland, where he baptized thousands of people and built hundreds of churches. Within a century, Saint Patrick turned Ireland from a pagan land to a mostly Christian land.

To remember Saint Patrick and honor Ireland, we celebrate Saint Patrick's Day on March 17 by eating Irish food—corned beef and cabbage—and wearing green—Ireland's color.

Part of the lore about Saint Patrick is that he chased the snakes out of Ireland, but that probably did not happen.

1. How do you think we started to have holidays of fun as well as of remembrance?
2. What makes some holidays important enough to get a day off but not others?

· · · · · · ·

Mother's Day

Mother's Day started nearly 150 years ago when a woman named Anna Jarvis organized a day to raise awareness of poor health conditions in her community. This was a cause she believed would be best supported by mothers, so she called it "Mother's Work Day." In 1905 her daughter, also named Anna, continued the crusade to honor the work of her mother.

Anna began to lobby prominent businessmen and Presidents Taft and Roosevelt to create a special day to honor mothers. Five years later, the House of Representatives adopted a resolution calling for officials of the federal government to wear white carnations on Mother's Day. In 1914 Anna's work resulted in the signing of a bill by Woodrow Wilson that recognized Mother's Day as a national holiday.

1. As you can tell by the story, Mother's Day has a deeper meaning than just buying a card or a gift. What do you think is the underlying message of this holiday?
2. Anna Jarvis tried to improve the poor living conditions in her community. In what ways could we help in our own community?
3. What can you do to honor your mother today? What other moms would you like to honor on this day?

Memorial Day

Memorial Day was first observed on May 30, 1868, and was known as Decoration Day. It was a special day set aside to honor the nation's Civil War dead by decorating their graves. During the first celebration of Decoration Day, General James Garfield made a speech at Arlington National Cemetery.

In 1966, President Lyndon Johnson declared Waterloo, New York, the official birthplace of Memorial Day. In 1971, Congress declared Memorial Day a national holiday to be celebrated the last Monday in May.

Memorial Day is celebrated each year at Arlington National Cemetery with a ceremony in which an American flag is placed on each grave. On that day, the president or vice president gives a speech honoring the contributions of people who died during war and lays a wreath at the Tomb of the Unknown Soldier.

1. Why do you suppose we honor soldiers who have died?
2. What would you like to learn about the Civil War that you don't already know?
3. What does it mean to honor someone?

....

Father's Day

William Smart, a Civil War veteran, was widowed when his wife died in childbirth with their sixth child. Although he was left with six children to raise alone, he did so with an inner strength and selflessness. One of his daughters,

Mrs. John B. Dodd, proposed the idea of a "father's day" in 1909 to honor the memory of her father.

As a result of her actions, the first Father's Day was observed on June 19, 1910, in Spokane, Washington. Fourteen years later, President Calvin Coolidge supported the idea of a national Father's Day. Fifty-six years after the first observation, President Lyndon Johnson signed a proclamation declaring the third Sunday of June as Father's Day.

1. How would you like to spend Father's Day?
2. Father's Day doesn't have to just include your own father. You can also honor your grandfather(s), uncle(s), or any other man you admire. Is there anyone else you would like to honor on Father's Day?
3. What does a father do that is special?

. . . .

Fourth of July

At the dinner table one night Mom asked, "What shall we do to celebrate the Fourth of July? Where do you think the best fireworks will be?"

Dad added, "I hope we'll be having fried chicken and watermelon. By the way, who knows why we have a holiday on the Fourth of July?"

The kids answered with, "So we can dress up in red, white, and blue," "So we can have a vacation," and "So we can have the cousins over and have a picnic."

Dad said, "Yes, we do all those things. But the real reason for the holiday is to celebrate our freedom. We were not always free. England was in charge of our country when we were colonies, and the British were not fair to the colonists. The British taxed the colonists without giving them a vote or letting them say how they wanted the country to be run.

"Our forefathers were very brave. They tried to work things out with the British, but Britain wouldn't give in. The colonists wrote the Declaration of Independence to explain to England why they wanted to be free, and it was adopted on July 4, 1776. We celebrate July 4 as our country's birthday."

1. Do you know another name for the Fourth of July?
2. What does "The Star-Spangled Banner" have to do with the Fourth of July?
3. What could we add to our Fourth of July celebration to remind us how grateful we are for our freedom?

· · · · · · ·

Labor Day

Labor Day originated in the town of Pullman, Illinois. George Pullman, president of a railroad sleeping car company, founded the town in 1880. Most of the residents of Pullman worked for the Pullman company.

However, when the Depression struck, many people lost their jobs; those who didn't lose their jobs found that their pay wasn't enough for rent and food. As a result, the employees went on strike and demanded lower rents and higher pay. Railroad workers across the country supported the Pullman employees and boycotted trains carrying Pullman cars.

President Grover Cleveland declared the strike a federal crime and ended the strike by sending twelve thousand troops to Pullman. Two of the protesters were killed.

Six days later, in an attempt to soothe the nation's workers, the president signed a bill to make Labor Day a national holiday.

1. What does it mean when employees go on strike?
2. What happened in the Depression?
3. Do you think it's important to have a holiday to celebrate workers?

. . . .

Columbus Day

Hundreds of years ago, sailing the seas was a dangerous undertaking. There were storms and pirates, but since people wanted to trade goods with other countries, sailors made the trip.

Christopher Columbus believed that he could find a new way to sail to Asia from Europe that would be safer and shorter. He knew the king and queen of Portugal, so he asked them for money to take three ships on this new route. King Ferdinand and Queen Isabella thought it could be profitable for them and funded the trip.

In 1492 Columbus and ninety men set sail on the flagship *Santa Maria*. Two other ships, the *Niña* and the *Pinta*, came with him. After sailing west for three months, Columbus saw the light signaling land where his maps indicated India. When he and his crew went ashore, they expected to see people native to India, so they called the first people they saw "Indians."

173

Hundreds of years later, Columbus was recognized for his discovery. In 1792, the city of Washington was officially named the District of Columbia and became the capital of the United States. In 1905, Colorado became the first state to observe a Columbus Day. Since 1971, it has been celebrated on the second Monday in October.

1. What do you suppose would have happened if Queen Isabella had refused to give Columbus the money?
2. What do you imagine it would have been like to be on a ship for three months during the time of Columbus?
3. Columbus was sure that he would find India on his journey. What do you suppose would make him think that?

· · · · · · ·

Thanksgiving

The English Pilgrims who founded America celebrated the first American Thanksgiving in 1621 with their Native American guests, who brought gifts of food as a gesture of goodwill. Eventually New Englanders began to celebrate Thanksgiving each year after the harvest.

The tradition of holding annual Thanksgiving holidays spread throughout New England and into other states. In 1817, New York State adopted Thanksgiving Day as an annual custom, and many other states soon did the same. Most of the state celebrations were held in November but not always on the same day.

In the mid-nineteenth century, Sarah Josepha Hale led a movement to establish Thanksgiving Day as a national holiday. During the Civil War, President Abraham Lincoln proclaimed the last Thursday in November to be Thanksgiving Day. After the war, Congress established it as a national holiday.

1. Thanksgiving Day has changed over the years, but it remains a day to reflect and be thankful. What are you most thankful for?
2. Being thankful is a good way to appreciate the gifts that God has given to you. If you were thankful every day for at least one gift, do you think you would be happier?
3. Let's select a gift to be thankful for today.

· · · · · · ·

Christmas

Christmas is based on the story of Jesus' birth as described in the Gospel of Matthew and the Gospel of Luke.

Although the Gospels describe Jesus' birth in detail, they never mention the date, so historians don't know exactly when he was born.

Roman Catholics first celebrated Christmas, then known as the Feast of the Nativity, as early as 336 A.D. They chose December 25 as the day for the Feast of the Nativity.

Scholars believe the frequently used shortened form of Christmas—Xmas—may have come into use in the thirteenth century. The X stands for the Greek letter *chi,* an abbreviation of *Khristos* (Christ), and also represents the cross on which Jesus was crucified.

According to legend, the Christmas tree tradition began with the founder of German Protestantism, Martin Luther. While walking through the forest on Christmas Eve, Luther was so moved by the beauty of the starlit fir trees that he brought one indoors and decorated it with candles to remind his children of God's creation.

1. What does Christmas mean to you?

2. Christmas is about celebrating the birth of Jesus Christ. How do you think we can celebrate his birth this year? Let's find something that we haven't done already.

3. How would you explain the true meaning of Christmas to someone who didn't know anything about Jesus?

Appendix

A Special Section about Safety

· · · · · · · · · · · · · · · · · · · ·

If your child has been at home with you from infancy, pre-school or kindergarten will be the first time he or she is away from your ever-vigilant eye. Safety issues now shift from keeping your little one out of the cleaning supplies to ensuring that your child is safe even when he or she is away from you. Although statistically the likelihood of your child being the victim of abuse at the hands of an adult is low, this is an emotionally "hot" issue for parents. Even though it may be terrifying for you to think about, discussing abuse with your child is crucial, because the more your child knows about staying safe, the safer he or she will be.

The rising awareness of crimes against children has left many families with a sense of fear. You and your child need to be careful and aware, but you do not need to be afraid. Talk to your child in a calm and reassuring manner, being careful not to discuss the frightening details of what might happen to a child who does not follow the safety guidelines.

The most important key to child safety is effective communication with your children. Children who do not feel that they are listened to or who do not think that their needs are met in the home are more vulnerable. The first step you should take is to establish an atmosphere in the home where your children feel truly comfortable discussing sensitive matters and relating experiences in which someone may have approached them in a way that made them feel uncomfortable. The simple truth is that children are often too afraid or confused to report their experiences and fears.

We tend to think of two general classes of abuse of children: physical abuse and sexual abuse Physical abuse is the easiest to detect because there are generally bruises or marks on the child's body. Sexual abuse can be trickier because perpetrators of abuse might warn or threaten a child to not tell anyone about what they are doing.

Some manifestations of abuse can simply be normal stages of development. For example, excessive masturbation can be a symptom of sexual abuse, but it is also normal for children to touch their genitals out of curiosity. When parents are worried about the possibility of their child having been abused, I encourage them to look at a global perspective of their child, not just one or two actions he or she might be doing. In other words, how is the child doing overall? Are there changes in sleeping or eating habits? Does the child have a tendency to be secretive? What kind of relationship does the child have with friends and family members?

Remember that the best protection for your child is preparation. When one of the teachers at our son's school discovered a man hiding in the bushes near the school, she immediately went into the predetermined safety drill. All the students were taken to a lockdown area. Once the children were safely in place, the police were called and arrived on the property within four minutes. Because of the preparation of the teachers and staff, most of the children were unaware of the incident, and the situation was controlled in a matter of minutes. Much like this, you will prepare your son or daughter to be safe in the world. Self-safety for your child is best accomplished over a period of time, not all at once in one frightening tale about scary people who are out to hurt them. The key here is to walk the line between caution and alarm.

We can begin the process of personal safety when our children are very young, by encouraging them to use the correct words for parts of their body. As a culture, we are often uncomfortable with being verbally explicit about the sexual parts of our body. Because of this discomfort, we tend to make up nicknames for genitals. However, our children need to know that they can talk to us about anything that is going on with their body, especially if someone is inappropriately touching a part of it. If we are candid about their bodies, they will in turn feel more secure about being open with us. We can begin a discussion by naming the parts of their bodies: "This is your knee; this is your toe; and this is your penis." This frankness will form the foundation for talks about personal areas and okay-touch and not okay-touch. Children should not be asked to touch anyone in the areas of their body that would be covered by a bathing suit or allow anyone to touch them in those areas.

"Stay away from strangers" is a popular warning to children to prevent abduction or exploitation. Many children, however, are abducted or exploited by people who are familiar with them but who may or may not be known to the children's parents. The term *stranger* suggests a concept that children do not understand and is one that ignores what we do know about the people who commit crimes against children. It misleads children into believing that they should only be aware of individuals who have an unusual or slovenly appearance. Instead, it is more appropriate to teach children to be on the lookout for certain kinds of *situations* or *actions* rather than certain kinds of individuals.

Children should be raised to be polite and friendly, but they need to know it is okay for them to be suspicious of any adult asking for assistance. Children help other children, but there is no need for them to be assisting adults. Often exploiters or abductors initiate a seemingly innocent contact with the victim. They may try to get to know the children and befriend them.

Parents must teach their children that they should stay away from individuals in cars or vans, and that it is okay for them to say no—even to an adult. Since most children are taught to respect adult authority, parents should explain why the child's personal safety is more important than being polite. Parents should also reinforce that there is always someone who can help them. A clear, calm, and reassuring message about situations and actions to look out for is easier for children to understand than a particular profile or image of a "stranger."

Here are some steps you can follow to ensure your children's safety:

- Know where your children are at all times; be familiar with their friends and daily activities.
- Be sensitive to changes in your children's behavior; they are a signal that you should talk to your children about what caused the changes.
- Be alert to a teenager or adult who is paying an unusual amount of attention to your children or giving them inappropriate or expensive gifts.
- Teach your children to trust their own feelings and assure them that they have the right to say no to what they sense is wrong.
- Listen to your children's fears and be supportive in all your discussions with them.
- Teach your children that no one should approach them or touch them in a way that makes them feel uncomfortable; stress that they should tell you immediately if someone does.
- Be careful about babysitters and any other individuals who care for your children; obtain references and try to access background screening information about these individuals. Many states give citizens access to sex-offender registries and criminal histories.

As soon as your children are old enough to understand, they can begin the process of learning how to protect themselves. Children must learn these basic rules:

- If you are in a public place and get separated from your parents, don't wander around looking for them. Go to a checkout counter, the security office, or the lost and found and tell the person in charge that you need help finding your parents.

- You should not get into a car or go anywhere with any person unless your parents have told you that it is okay.

- If someone follows you on foot or in a car, stay away from him or her. You should not get close to any car unless your parent or a trusted adult accompanies you.

- Grown-ups and others who need help should not be asking children for help; they should be asking older people.

- No one should be asking you for directions or for help in looking for a lost puppy or telling you that your mother or father is in trouble and that he or she will take you to them.

- If someone you don't know tries to take you somewhere, quickly get away from him (or her) and yell, "This man (woman) is trying to take me away" or "This person is not my father (mother)."

- You should never go places alone; try to take a friend with you.

- Always ask your parents' permission to leave the yard or play area or to go into someone's home.

- Never hitchhike or try to get a ride home with anyone unless your parents have told you it is okay to ride with the person.

- If someone you don't know wants to take your picture, tell him or her no and tell your parents or teacher.

- No one should touch any part of your body that would be covered by a bathing suit, nor should you touch anyone else in those areas. Your body is special and private.

- You can be assertive; you have the right to say no to someone who tries to take you somewhere, touches you, or makes you feel uncomfortable, scared, or confused in any way.

Children should not be forced to give affection to an adult or teenager if they do not want to. Be alert to signs that your child is trying to avoid someone and listen carefully when your child tells you how he or she feels about someone. The reality of sexual exploitation is that often the child is very confused, uncomfortable, and unwilling to talk about the experience to parents, teachers, or anyone else. But if you have established an atmosphere of trust and support in your home, your child will feel free to talk without fear of accusation, blame, or guilt. Parents should be alert to these indicators of sexual abuse:

- Changes in behavior, extreme mood swings, withdrawal, fearfulness, and excessive crying
- Bed-wetting, nightmares, fear of going to bed, or other sleep disturbances
- Acting out inappropriate sexual activity or showing an unusual interest in sexual matters
- A sudden acting out of feelings or aggressive or rebellious behavior
- Regression to infantile behavior
- A fear of certain places, people, or activities, especially being alone with certain people
- Pain, itching, bleeding, fluid, or rawness in the private areas.

Shopping with your children can pose different challenges. Here are some guidelines for safe shopping:

- When in a public facility, always supervise your children, and always accompany young children to the rest room. Make certain your children know they must stay with you at all times while shopping.

- Arrange to have your older children meet you in a predetermined spot (such as the sales counter of the last store you were in or the mall's information booth) should they become separated from you while shopping. Teach younger children to look for people who can be sources of help, such as a uniformed security officer, a salesperson with a name tag, the person in the information booth, or a uniformed law-enforcement officer. Stress that they should never leave the store or mall to go looking for you.

- Make visits to the mall opportunities for your children to practice safe-shopping skills; teach them how to use a public telephone and how to locate adult sources of help within the mall or a store. Practice having them check first with you before going anywhere within a mall or store. Leave clothing with your children's names displayed at home, as it can bring about attention from inappropriate people who may be looking for an opportunity to start a conversation with your children.

- Do not leave children alone at public facilities such as video arcades, movie theaters, or playgrounds as a convenient babysitter while you are holiday shopping. Never leave children in toy or specialty stores and expect store personnel to supervise and care for them.

- If you allow your older children to go to the mall without you, insist that they take a friend; it's more fun and much safer. Tell them to stay together and never to enter a rest room alone. They should also check in with you on a regular basis while they are out. Make certain they know when and where you will pick them up and what to do in case plans change.

184

Nothing takes the place of your supervision when you are in a public place with your children. If you are going shopping and feel that you will be distracted, make arrangements to have someone else care for your children.

References

Bandura, A. (1986). *Social foundations of thought and action.* Englewood Cliffs, NJ: Prentice-Hall.

Bloom, B. J. (Ed.). (1956). *Taxonomy of educational objectives: The classification of educational goals, by a committee of college and university examiners.* New York: Longmans, Green.

Chapman, G. D., & Campbell, R. (1997). *The five love languages of children.* Chicago: Moody.

Miller, P. H. (1989). *Theories of developmental psychology* (2nd ed.). New York: Freeman.

Kelly Lingerfeldt Stille, Psy.D., is a child psychologist who has worked with the Solano County Youth and Family Services, Kaiser Permanente, and with the Child Protection Center of the University of California Davis Medical Center. She is a professor of psychology at Napa Valley Community College, conducts community parenting workshops, and is the mother of four, including twins.

Patricia Wachter, Ed.D., is a former school counselor and teacher, a licensed educational psychologist, and a marriage and family therapist in Napa, California. She and Kelly, her daughter, also developed a two-minute TV show called *The Parent Doctor*, which is being considered for syndication.